Read Jan '2017.

THE
NEW CIVIC
RELIGION

A CHRISTIAN STUDY
GUIDE TO HUMANISM

THE
NEW CIVIC
RELIGION

A CHRISTIAN STUDY
GUIDE TO HUMANISM

PATRICK SOOKHDEO

The New Civic Religion: A Christian Study Guide to Humanism

First edition, May 2016

Published in the United States by Isaac Publishing
6729 Curran Street, McLean, Virginia 22101

Copyright © 2016 Patrick Sookhdeo

Library of Congress Control Number: 2016941693

ISBN: 978-0-9967245-9-3

Printed in the United Kingdom

CONTENTS

A Christian Way Forward

Resources

  • Five Key Humanist Documents
  • Letter from US Departments of Education and Justice
    dated May 13, 2016

HOW TO USE THIS BOOK

The first eleven chapters of this book give an overview of humanism and the new civic religion, which are posing a serious challenge to the Church in many countries today. The focus is on countries where this challenge is furthest advanced, such as the UK and USA, but it is hoped that the book will be useful to Christians in many other parts of the world, and may enable them to discern likely future developments in their own country and perhaps to respond to the challenge at a much earlier stage. Bearing in mind that there may be readers all around the globe, this book has been written in a simple, everyday style of English (as much as this is possible with a complex subject matter).

The remaining chapters provide resources for readers who wish to study the subject in more depth.

Chapter 12 lists some practical suggestions for how Christians can respond to the challenge of humanism and the new civic religion.

Chapter 13 provides material for those who would like to reflect from a Biblical perspective on the information in chapters 1 to 12 and to ponder some of the issues raised in these chapters. For each of the twelve main chapters, there is a short Bible study and some discussion questions related both to the chapter and to the Bible passage. The questions are designed partly to help readers make sure they have grasped the main points of each chapter, partly to help them consider the relevance to their own situation and context, partly to help them apply the Bible's teaching to the issues in the chapter, and partly to suggest issues which need careful thought and consideration. This material could be used by an individual or a small group. It could also be used in a more formal training session in which a leader takes students through the book chapter by chapter, finishing each session with the relevant Bible study and using the questions to encourage a group discussion.

Chapter 14 gives an overview of evidence to support the authority, reliability and infallibility of the Bible, the Word of God.

Chapter 15 gives the text of two historic Christian creeds.

Finally there is a glossary and a list of references and sources including some key humanist documents.

1
INTRODUCTION -
THE NEW CIVIC RELIGION

"Although ... we have a very large Christian population, we do not consider ourselves a Christian nation or a Jewish nation or a Muslim nation; we consider ourselves a nation of citizens who are bound by ideals and a set of values."

US President Barack Obama, 2009

Since the Second World War, Western societies have been undergoing a transformation. From societies founded on Biblical principles and resting on a Christian foundation they are changing to societies resting on humanism and a civic religion with its own theology, ideology and morality. This has resulted in the gradual erosion not just of faith but also of a Christian moral basis.

Following mass killing by so-called Christian nations in two world wars and the gross inhumanity against Jews in the Holocaust, questions began to be raised about the validity of societies based on Christian principles. If Christians can do such things to each other and commit such horrendous crimes against Jews, then what use, people asked, was Christianity? New ideas began to be explored about Christianity, other religions and the wider world.

> **Karl Rahner** (1904-1984), a German Jesuit priest, believed in "anonymous Christians" by which he meant that non-Christians who behaved like Christians had God's grace at work in their lives and would gain salvation.
>
> **Wilfred Cantwell Smith** (1916-2000), a minister in the United Church of Canada and a professor at Harvard University, questioned the whole concept of religion, saying it was a relatively recent European idea, not a universal, worldwide idea. He wrote a book called *The Meaning and End of Religion* (1962).
>
> **Don Cupitt** (born 1934), a British Anglican priest and a lecturer at the University of Cambridge, has described himself as a Christian non-realist because he does not believe that God and Christ are real. His 1984 book *The Sea of Faith* challenged traditional Christian belief and led to a Sea of Faith movement whose aim is to "explore and promote religious faith as a human creation". He sees traditional faith as ebbing away.

These new ideas marginalised traditional Christian belief in favour of a pluralist multi-dimensional type of Christianity. Furthermore, a new civic religion was gradually developed to replace Christianity at the state level. President Obama described America in 2009 as a nation whose people were bound together by ideals and values, but not by Christianity or any other religion. This civic religion, which has its own moral and ethical values and no belief in the supernatural, lies at the heart of humanism.

THE CONCEPT OF JUDEO-CHRISTIANITY – HOW IT BEGAN AND WHERE IT HAS LED

In his essay *The Strange Short Career of Judeo-Christianity* (22 March 2016), Gene Zubovich, writes on how a liberal Church, influenced by a humanist culture and ideology, has allowed the Christian moral framework, which had shaped Western societies for centuries, to be watered down. In America during the Second World War it began to be popular for Christians to celebrate the similarities between Christian and Jewish morals and values. This was done mostly as an act of solidarity with and support for Jewish people in light of the atrocities being committed by the Nazis against the Jews. In this way the idea of a Judeo-Christian moral heritage and identity was created.

Zubovich goes on to explain that what started off with good intentions has now been taken too far. Recently it has become popular to expand the Judeo-Christian value system to include the moral values of the Islamic religion. Church leaders often try to find common ground between the three religions, sometimes called the Abrahamic religions. However, Christianity and Islam differ very much from each other in their moral teaching. Therefore, in order to find common ground with Muslims, Christian leaders have compromised on many of the core beliefs and fundamental values of Christianity.

Even more recently some Christians have started to speak about a common value system that Christians, Jews and Muslims share with people who have no religious belief. The quotation from President Obama at the beginning of this chapter is one example. It is a general trend in many Western churches that a civic moral system is being promoted by the Church at the expense of Christian core beliefs.

HOW CIVIC RELIGION DEVELOPED IN AMERICA

America's civil religion was established at its Founding and is spelled out in the Declaration of Independence (1776). It was theistic and non-sectarian for the simple reason that the organised political system of America was made up of a variety of religious groups, all of which wished for freedom of religion. However, the American Founding can only be understood in terms of the Christian context in which it took place.

On 28 June 1813 John Adams, the second president of the United States, wrote a letter to Thomas Jefferson, the principal author of the Declaration of Independence, about the basic principles on which the Founders achieved independence. President Adams asked: "And what were these principles? I answer, the general principles of Christianity in which all those sects were united and the general principles of English and American liberty in which all these young men united... Now I will avow that I then believed and now believe that those general principles of Christianity are as eternal and immutable as the existence and attributes of God. And that those principles of liberty are as unalterable as human nature... I could, therefore, safely say consistently with all my then and present information, that I believe they would never make discoveries in contradiction to these general principles." America understood itself in these terms well into the twentieth century, especially in respect to its struggles against the two forms of totalitarianism – Nazism and communism.

But the American civil religion has now changed. As moral and cultural relativism (or subjectivism) became accepted, so confidence was lost in the objective truth of the "eternal and immutable" principles of Christianity. This loss can be seen in *The Audacity of Hope*, Barack Obama's book written in 2006 before he became president, in which he stated: "Implicit in [the Constitution's] structure, in the very idea of ordered liberty, was a rejection of absolute truth, the infallibility of any idea or ideology or theology or 'ism', and any tyrannical consistency that might block future generations into a single, unalterable course." In other words, Obama is saying that, the truth does not set you free; the truth enslaves you. According to this argument, it is necessary to reject objective truth in order to have freedom. Gone are the "laws of Nature and of Nature's God" (as described in the Declaration of Independence) on which the United States was founded. Humanism is their replacement.

The American civil religion has now been transformed into a weapon against the very truths that made it possible. The state is now being used to enforce the doctrines of humanism.

This is being replicated in many other countries, creating situations where the government controls all the religions through an overarching civic religion that effectively side-lines God and puts humans at the centre. C.S. Lewis had warned in 1943 that such moral subjectivism "must be the destruction of the society which accepts it". If people believe there is no such thing as objective truth or objective morality, then they do not teach virtue to their children. Worse still, they tell their children there is no such thing as virtue. This erodes both the practical and the theoretical foundations of democracy and free government. With each person "a law unto himself", anarchy is the logical result. Anarchy will swiftly be replaced by tyranny because, as Robert R. Reilly (1983, p. 21) says, "People have always shown their preference for despotism over disorder."

HUMANISM

The collapse of Christian morality in society has been partly the result of deliberate, orchestrated and intentional humanist efforts, subtle yet aggressively effective. This "humanist missionary movement" is described in chapter 5.

Humanism believes that there is no God and so it is up to humans to save themselves by creating their own morals and way of living. Unlike Christianity, humanism teaches that humans are by nature good. Humanism does not say anything about a fallen nature that needs to be redeemed, Humanism also holds that moral standards that are right for some people in some situations may be wrong for other people in other situations. This is called "situational ethics". There is no God to guide or command, so there are no absolute rights and wrongs. People can and should choose how they live and cannot be blamed for what they do. There is no such thing as sin in humanism (except the "sin" of believing in God). Humanists believe that everything can be explained by science and rational thought.

Not all atheists and humanists are actively opposed to religion. Some even recognise and affirm the value of Christian morals and the positive effect they have had on society, and wish to see these moral values continue. However, fundamentalist atheist and humanist movements have emerged whose beliefs and activities are as extreme as those associated with the worst forms of religious extremism. This fundamentalist type of humanism opposes the Christian way of living, and seeks to remove all religious influence from society, especially Christian influence. Such humanists consider that formal religion is not only senseless but also dangerous to the existence of humankind. They say that if humanity is to evolve, all forms of religion must be abolished, as religion prevents intellectual, social and scientific development. They also believe that religion causes divisions, violence and wars.

> **Humanism as defined by the International Humanist and Ethical Union (bylaw 5.1)**
> Humanism is a democratic and ethical life stance, which affirms that human beings have the right and responsibility to give meaning and shape to their own lives. It stands for the building of a more humane society through an ethic based on human and other natural values in the spirit of reason and free inquiry through human capabilities. It is not theistic, and it does not accept supernatural views of reality.

TURNING HUMANS INTO GOD

The common experience of human beings is to desire happiness but to be unhappy. They feel a keen sense of loss and desolation. They seek, but find nothing in this world that meets their deepest longings. They suffer and die. Thus humans have always been confronted with the fact of evil. Even if they do not call it "evil" they admit there is something seriously wrong with the world. The Christian tradition shaped the West by teaching that the source of evil in the world is "original sin", which Robert R. Reilly (1983 p. 9) has described as "a cataclysmic dislocation in the relationship between God and man which resulted in 'fallen nature'". The essence of this original sin is pride, that is, the human preference for oneself instead of God.

Humanism tries to solve the problem of evil, here in this world, without God. Making a deliberate choice (not a reasoned decision) to disbelieve in God's existence, they hope that humans – without God to hinder and restrict them – will be able to rise higher than they could if they believed in God. As Karl Marx said, "The religion of the workers has no God, because it seeks to restore the divinity of man."

But as Christians, we know that human beings, although sinful, are made in the image of God their creator. Those who reject the idea of God, reject the idea of His divine image in humans. Therefore they lose all understanding of humans and how they reflect the character of God. Humans are considered nothing more than animals.

Discussion For and Against

"Man – the master of the world – does not bear any evil within himself, and all the defects of life are caused by misguided social systems which must therefore be corrected."

Alexander Solzhenitsyn (1978)

"Where there is no God, there is no man."

Nicholas Berdyaev (1933)

"Unless there is a being superior to man, nothing in theory prevents some men from degrading other men to the level of subhuman."

Paul Eidelberg (1977)

"The attempted deification of man has backfired into the charnel houses and slave camps of the various Gulags. Those aspiring to be gods have become worse than animals. The great hope of nihilism was that 'man will rise higher when he ceases to flow into god.' But in God's absence, the distinction dissolves not only between God and man, but also between man and animal."

Robert R. Reilly (1983, p. 16)

HOW HUMANISM AFFECTS SOCIETY AND THE CHURCH

To an uninformed observer, humanism may appear quite harmless but the effects it has had on society have been dramatic and significant. Humanism has become so firmly embedded within society that people do not have to be followers of humanism or even to know what it is to have been influenced by it. Within formerly Christian contexts, humanism is actively promoting a society where morality is negotiable and Christian values are questioned, challenged, or even rejected. Individuals pursue pleasure rather than righteousness. Behaviours that are contrary to God's laws and Christian values are at first permitted, and then celebrated.

One result of this is that the old concept of truth and truthful living has almost vanished. Brenda Watson (2014, p. 77) notes that "truth" has become a negative word for some people, because they see it used as an excuse for being obstinate, intolerant, hostile and even violent. Others consider truth to be an impossible ideal that can never be reached. Watson says that "postmodernist thinking . . . sees especially institutional truth-claiming as little more than power politics – a way for people to maintain their ownership, status and sense of being right."

But even back in the nineteenth century, the same idea had already arisen. The German philosopher Friedrich Nietzche (1844-1900) proclaimed, "We have abolished the world of truth" and "Nothing is true". If truth has been abolished, then the two main routes to discovering truth, that is reason and revelation, become irrelevant. Nietzche's belief that all values are baseless, reason is useless, and nothing can be known is called nihilism.

Institutional corruption is another result of the rise of humanism. Scandals abound, affecting the political, media and other civic institutions. Money, power and sexual abuse are some of the recurring themes, resulting in a loss of trust.

The moral collapse of many civic institutions is now being reflected in the Church as well, across Orthodox, Catholic, Protestant, Anglican and evangelical denominations. Here too it results in a loss of trust. There are frequent cases of financial corruption, power intrigues and sexual sin. Power, which drives political, military and other leaders, now equally seems to drive Christian leaders as they compete to build their own ministry empires. Sections of the Christian media (especially those publishing online) have sunk to the level of the worst examples of the secular media, using the pretext of "public interest" to excuse what they are doing. The result is unverified reporting and character assassinations, often expressed in a vocabulary that brings no glory to God.

A value-free society

Under the influence of humanism, many people seek a value-free society. Brenda Watson (2014, pp. 30-34) explains that the idea of "value-free" began with scientists who wanted to study their data objectively, without making value-judgements. It was especially used by sociologists and anthropologists who did not want to make judgements about whether the beliefs of the people they were studying were true or false. But when value-free becomes a goal for society as a whole, there are problems. Watson says that a fact/belief divide lies at the root of the value-free society. Values are not seen as based on the fact of the character of God, things for humans to discover rather than create. Instead, values are considered to be mere opinions. So in pluralist societies the emphasis is not on truth but on the right to hold an opinion. Values, including moral values, are considered to have no real existence. Thus there is a situation of moral relativism, in which right and wrong, good and evil, are considered purely human concepts, flexible and adaptable according to human wishes and needs, useful as someone travels through life, useful for enabling societies to thrive, but without any other reality. (Furedi, 2004, p. 4)

The humanist desire to equalise every individual within society and to equalise the value of everyone's opinion can become a hindrance or even destructive. It can create hostility towards leaders or to anyone who shines at anything. In countries like the UK, Australia, New Zealand and Canada it is called the "tall poppy syndrome". In China and Japan there is a similar saying that the nail which stands out will get hammered down. Other people talk about a "crab mentality" referring to the way crabs in a bucket pull down whichever one rises to the top of the pile, so that none of them manage to escape.

All these phrases refer to a situation where people with genuine talents and abilities, which make them stand out from the crowd or lift them to positions of high status, are not respected or admired. Instead other people resent them, criticise them and attack them to try to bring them down. Leaders in every sphere of society are likely to be targeted, and this attitude is seeping into the Church. It is creating a crisis in leadership, as people increasingly fear to rise to prominent positions, while those already in leadership roles are paralysed and dare not act for fear of attack. There is a danger that those with huge personal ambition could soon dominate the leadership scene, even if their talents are only mediocre, as others dare not move into key positions of responsibility.

The growing concern for equality has been helpful in supporting the right of women to be treated as equals of men. This was very necessary to correct an unjust imbalance in which women were suffering. However, the trend has continued past the point of equality to a situation where women in the West now have a better lot in life than men, yet continue to play the victim. This at least is the analysis of the British author Fay Weldon (2016), who has a longstanding association with the feminist movement. She has even suggested that a reason why some men are changing themselves into women by transgender surgery is because of the superior position of women in society: "The only way men have of fighting back against the natural superiority of women is by becoming women themselves."

In the Western Church, over the same few decades, there has been a growing feminisation, One part of this is the increasing number of women in Christian leadership roles, which is to be welcomed. However, as in society, the trend now appears to have gone so far that it is beginning to become destructive. The great spiritual gifts of women are sometimes being used for selfish and negative purposes. Some people have spoken of a "Jezebel spirit" developing in the Church, as women become increasingly dominant. This refers to Jezebel the wife of King Ahab, who took the lead in many evil acts and showed herself to be manipulative, greedy and cruel (1 Kings 18-21).

Humanism supposedly promotes freedom. Yet many freedoms, especially religious freedom, are being removed from societies where humanism is influential. In countries where humanism is strong, people trying to live out a Christian life according to the law of God are increasingly being marginalised, harassed or even persecuted. In some instances Christian groups have been sued or had criminal proceedings initiated against them for practising and promoting Christian values. Christians who challenge the humanist way of life are branded as judgemental bigots and extremists.

CHURCHES AND CHRISTIANS HAVE BEEN INFLUENCED BY HUMANISM

In 1963 Harry Blamires wrote a book called *The Christian Mind* saying there was no longer a Christian mind, for Christian people no longer thought in a Christian way. He saw that, with the rise of humanism, the Christian mind was being shaped into a secular mind and that the result of this would be Christians embracing secular values. Some churches and Christians are now living lives that are effectively humanist and focused on money, materialism and pleasure. Some people use the phrases "practical atheist" or "Christian atheist" to describe this type of Christian. Not only Christian but also Jewish voices have pointed out the void created when love of money becomes the main principle of life. "On what, if anything is our civilisation based?" asked Bishop Richard Harries (2008, p. 174). "Has Europe lost its soul to the markets?" asked Rabbi Jonathan Sacks (2011, p. 22).

In Christian theology there have been further developments which have also influenced Christian behaviour. One example is the doctrine of hyper-grace, which rightly promotes God's unconditional love for us but wrongly does not deal with the issue of sin or challenge individuals to live righteously. As a result many Christians live lives that are contrary to His will. Behaviour such as cohabitation of couples before marriage, sleeping around, dressing immodestly, pornography, abortion, accepting and paying bribes, drunkenness, divorce, disloyalty, lying, deception and false accusation are acceptable and widely practised.

"There is no longer a Christian mind. It is a commonplace that the mind of modern man has been secularized. For instance, it has been deprived of any orientation towards the supernatural. Tragic as this fact is, it would not be so desperately tragic had the Christian mind held out against the secular drift. But unfortunately the Christian mind has succumbed to the secular drift with a degree of weakness and nervelessness unmatched in Christian history."

Harry Blamires, *The Christian Mind,* (1963, p. 3)

Another development in Christian theology which has been encouraged by humanism is that of universalism and postmodernism. Universalism is the belief that all religions lead to God, while postmodernists believe there are no absolute rights or wrongs and everyone can and should choose what they believe and how they live. Many churches within these contexts are hesitant to preach the Gospel as described in John 14:6: "I am the way and the truth and the life. No-one comes to the Father except through me." Their hesitation stems from a strong feeling that such views could be offensive to people of other faiths. Perhaps some Christians even believe that there may be other roads to God and, therefore, it is not for Christianity to be so narrow-minded or prescriptive. Also there is increasing rejection of the idea of judgement. This makes some Christians reluctant to challenge the views and practices of other religions. For example, there are elements of other religions and ideologies that should be questioned and confronted. And so commitment to truth, righteousness, justice and the preaching of the Gospel is being compromised.

Many conservative evangelical British Christians were startled in 2006 when Joel Edwards, the General Director of the Evangelical Alliance of the UK, wrote in an article that there would be a good impact if every church invited a Muslim cleric to its worship service to teach the congregation about Islam. He later affirmed this view in a personal letter and in his 2008 book *An Agenda for Change*.

THE CHURCH IS LOSING ITS RELEVANCE

Christianity is retreating. This is partly as a result of humanist attacks and partly because it is allowing humanist culture to override Kingdom values. The Church no longer appears to have a relevant and authoritative voice within society. It is right that State and Church should be separate from each other. However, the Christian community should still seek to influence leaders and state agents and to provide a moral framework for society. As the Church and God are pushed out of the public space, governments are becoming all-powerful and increasingly seek to control more and more areas of people's lives. Christian principles can help governments to make good, wise and just decisions and laws.

THE STATE INTERFERING IN THE AFFAIRS OF THE CHURCH

In many countries, the State is using civic religion as a means to gain more control. Humanism has therefore been given a primary position in guiding the ethical basis of society. As mentioned earlier, one important aspect of this is the humanist belief that religion of any kind causes conflict and war. And so, in order to create a safe society, governments are re-interpreting religions and setting the moral and ethical criteria for society. For example, governments desire to control the spread of Islamic extremism, but in an effort not to single out just one religion, such governments impose controls on all religions. They use the pretext of security to monitor, regulate and disempower Christian groups.

A UK prison chaplain

At the beginning of 2016 in the United Kingdom, a Christian chaplain working in a prison was banned from praying with inmates and sharing the Christian faith with them. His future sermons were to be monitored and censored. It is feared that the precedent that this case set will allow the State to determine what is said in any church in the country. And so Christians who challenge the decisions and injustices of a state can be marginalised and in some instances censored, fined, removed from their jobs or positions or even arrested.

CONCLUSION

Humanism is a real and widespread threat not only to Christianity but to humankind as a whole. A new type of civic religion has emerged throughout society and even within the Church. It has a worldview and culture that marginalises Christian doctrine and focuses instead on a civic moral code, much of which is in opposition to Christian morality.

The humanist, civic religion has permeated society and is now firmly entrenched in modern culture, even in sections of the Church. Some churches and Christians have embraced humanist culture to such a degree that their loyalties lie more with the civic religion and with a humanist government and society than with the Kingdom of God. Christianity is in danger and in a state of moral crisis.

2
HISTORICAL INFLUENCES ON HUMANISM

The term "humanism" is relatively new. It has only been used formally since the nineteenth century. However, the concepts and philosophy of humanism have been around for centuries.

INDIAN AND EASTERN INFLUENCES

Many movements or philosophies have had influences on modern day humanism. One of the earliest humanist movements recorded was the Lokayata system founded in India around 1500 BC. This materialistic system rejected the notion of God, gods, or a creator. Later in India, in the sixth century BC, it became more widespread as more and more Indian thinkers began to question the existence of God, the supernatural, and the authority of the Hindu religious texts called Vedas. There have been many variations of the Lokayata system. Among the most popular is Carvaka whose followers believe that only the natural world exists. They argue that life must be lived to the full and humans must pursue happiness and pleasure above all else. Other movements focus on the superiority of humans. Others focus on choosing their own morality and way of living. People were taught that the only power they could rely on was themselves and that they must, therefore, look within themselves for wisdom, guidance and morality.

Another Indian influence on the humanism philosophy is Theravada Buddhism. This religion rejects the concept of a creator God or considers it irrelevant. Its followers revere Buddha, "the awakened one", but only as a wise human teacher, not as God. They see him as a model of a fully enlightened person. Virtue is considered very important, with many detailed rules based on the principles of no killing, stealing, sexual misconduct, lying or use of intoxicants. But people have free will to do right or wrong. Each individual is on a journey of enlightenment to Nirvana (bliss) and the way to achieve this is to extinguish belief in a separate self, so as to get rid of all desires. Until this happens an individual is doomed to repeated rebirth. (Mahayana Buddhism is theistic, unlike Theravada Buddhism.)

During the 1960s and 1970s many of these Indian philosophies were incorporated into the modern humanist way of thinking.

CHINA AND CONFUCIUS

In China, a form of humanism began to emerge through the philosopher Confucius (551-479 BC). He stated that human values, rather than the supernatural, should govern our lives. He promoted what has become known as the *Silver Rule*: "One should not treat others in ways that one would not like to be treated." Confucius' teachings were very popular and had a large impact on early Chinese culture and worldview. During the European periods of the Renaissance and Enlightenment (see pages 21-24) early promoters of humanist philosophy began to use Confucius and Eastern philosophies to try and bring down the Church. They argued that Chinese people were civilised, intelligent, moral and ethical, and they were not Christian, so clearly God and the Church are not needed for morality or civilisation.

ANCIENT GREECE AND ROME (900 BC - 500 AD)

Ancient Greece is often regarded as the birthplace of modern Western thought, culture and philosophy. Ideas from this time have had a large impact on modern humanism. In ancient Greece much of life was explained through myths, legends and the involvement of gods. Greek thinkers began to question these explanations and tried to find more logical and provable reasons for how the world and universe worked. Not all Greek philosophers were atheists but they did teach people to question things. Greek scholars had new ideas about astronomy, mathematics, anatomy, natural and physical laws, and also considered ethics, morality and how humans interact. The world's first democracy was established in Athens in the sixth century BC. Many teachers and thinkers began to gain large followings, such as Thales, Plato, Socrates and Aristotle. Humanists state that one of the most influential Greek philosophers was Epicurus (341-271 BC) who taught that humans can live good lives independent of any religion or gods. He also taught that pleasure and pain were the only measures of good and evil. He proposed that pleasure must be pursued and pain avoided.

Another important ancient Greek philosophy was Stoicism, developed about 300 BC by Zeno. It gained many followers in ancient Rome as well as Greece and was popular for over five centuries. It has had a profound influence on the West even until modern times. Stoics believed in a self-controlled and virtuous life-style, lived in accordance with nature, which they equated with God. They taught that people should maintain an inner calm and avoid destructive emotions, no matter what their external situation was (pain or pleasure, poverty or wealth, sickness or health). Seneca and Epictetus taught that virtue is all you need to be happy. Stoics believed only in the existence of material things (including God as something material) and in the importance of reason. They also held that truth is what we come to believe because of what we feel through our senses; they did not believe in objective truth.

The Greeks created a form of education, which they believed would bring out the best in those being taught. This education was called *paideia* and included subjects such as philosophy, logic, rhetoric, grammar, mathematics, astronomy, literature, and drama. Later the Romans used the same model as the foundation of Roman education, and translated *paideia* into the Latin *studia humanitas* (the study of humanity).

The Roman Empire began to decline and by the sixth century AD it had fallen. But Christianity spread across Europe from its base in the Middle East and North Africa.

THE EUROPEAN MIDDLE AGES 500 - 1500

Over the next thousand years the Church (both Orthodox and Catholic) became more and more powerful, especially since, in the West, it was the only governing structure left standing after the collapse of the Roman Empire. It was involved in the functioning of governments, and individuals who challenged the power of the Church, or Church tradition, were often severely punished. Most Christians will agree that during this time there were parts of the established Church that were misguided and acted against what Jesus taught.

ISLAMIC INFLUENCE

During Islam's "Golden Age" (seventh to thirteenth centuries AD), while it was expanding across the Middle East, North Africa, South Asia and into parts of Europe, some Muslim scholars became interested in the humanist ideas and philosophies as well as the scientific and mathematical works of the early Greeks and Romans. They preserved these records in well-kept libraries across the Islamic world and translated them into Arabic. Meanwhile, medieval Europe had lost touch with classical learning of the past. There were even some Muslim scholars who began to question the existence of God. Eventually European scholars became interested in the scholarly works preserved by Muslims in Arabic, translated them, and began to explore the humanist philosophies.

THE RENAISSANCE 1350-1600

A great reawakening of classical learning began in Europe in the middle of the fourteenth century and later became known as the Renaissance (French for "rebirth"). During the Renaissance scholars returned to the *paideia* and *studia humanitas* ways of thinking, learning and teaching of the ancient Greeks and Romans. It was a time of great intellectual exploration. Scholars, artists and scientists of this time include Leonardo da Vinci, Michelangelo and Galileo. It is often thought that the Church was against this reawakening but in many instances Church leaders strongly supported intellectual development.

During the Renaissance a movement began in northern Italy that was later called humanism. In the Middle Ages only a narrow circle of scholarly clergy had discussed intellectual matters. The aim of the Renaissance humanists was to find a way to communicate ideas to a wider public and turn the ideas into action. The humanists looked back to Ancient Rome to find out how to communicate effectively, and went on to develop a great interest in the classical world, both Greek and Roman. They were very concerned about the accuracy of the ancient texts and translations. Humanism spread from Italy across Europe. Its motto may be the statement by Pico della Mirandola (1463-1494) that "man is the measure of all things".

The next stage was the development of Biblical humanism (also called Christian humanism), which applied these humanist attitudes to Christianity and looked very carefully at the Bible texts. The Biblical humanists emphasised tolerance, Christian love and individual moral responsibility. They tried to understand the Bible's real message so that people could lead truly Christian lives, and they promoted better education.

It is rather confusing that the word "humanism" is used to describe this Renaissance movement interested in classical studies and education as well as the very different movement that began in the nineteenth century and continues today, which this book is mainly about. The term "Christian humanism" is also used in two very different ways. It can mean the Renaissance group described in the paragraph above or it can mean modern Christian humanists who have different beliefs, placing less emphasis on the authority of the Bible and seeing morality as more relative (see chapter 4).

THE REFORMATION: SIXTEENTH CENTURY

During the sixteenth century, a number of Christian reformations swept across Europe. Two of the most well-known are the Reformation in Germany, led by Martin Luther, who had been influenced by the Christian humanists, and the Reformation in England, which was linked to Henry VIII's decision - for his own personal and political reasons - to break away from the authority of the Pope. Before the Reformation the Church was a very dominant power, and controlled many aspects of peoples' lives including their access to scripture. The Bible was read to people in Latin, which most of them could not understand. Many church leaders were corrupt and immoral.

The Reformation created a new kind of Christianity in Europe, which came to be called Protestantism. This emphasised the individual and taught that each believer could approach God directly, without needing a priest. It also emphasised the Bible more than church tradition and church authority. Thanks to the printing press and Bible translations, many people could read the Bible for themselves in their own language.

Many of the great thinkers of the time were inspired by their Christian faith and often saw themselves as studying two books: the book of God's words (the Bible) and the book of God's works (creation). They include such famous scientists as Francis Bacon who developed the "scientific method" of empirical experiments; John Napier who invented logarithms and also wrote on the book of Revelation; and Johannes Kepler whose works on planetary motion were motivated by an awe of God as the creator of the universe.

Many Christians believe that the Church today is in desperate need of another Reformation where the authority of God and His Word is restored as the central focus of the Church.

THE ENLIGHTENMENT: MID-SEVENTEENTH CENTURY TO LATE EIGHTEENTH CENTURY

As science and other studies developed, Europe moved into a time known as the Enlightenment. Everything had to be tested by reason or it could not be believed. Reason was supreme over revelation and tradition.

It was also a time when the concept of tolerance was explored. During the Renaissance and Reformation there had been terrible persecution of some of those trying to introduce new ideas, who were imprisoned, tortured or killed in horrible ways. But in the Enlightenment people started talking about the right to be able to express beliefs and ideas.

The idea of the separation of Church and State was promoted by many, and became especially important in America. (See chapter 5.)

Scottish thinkers played a significant role in the Enlightenment, for example, David Hume (1711-76), who denied both Christianity and natural law. (The concept of natural law says that humans can gain some knowledge of what is ethically good behaviour simply by using their own reason, that is, without any revelation from God.) In 1767 a Scottish philosopher, Adam Ferguson, published a book called *An Essay on the History of Civil Society* which traced humankind's progress from barbarism to social and political refinement. He saw society as the source of human morals and actions. It may be because of this heritage that Scotland is now considered by some to be the most secular part of the UK, which is held to be the most secular country in Europe.

The Swiss-born French philosopher Jean-Jacques Rousseau (1712-1778) wrote an essay entitled *Discourse on the Origin and Foundations of Inequality among Men.* In this he stated that the cause of the evils afflicting humankind is society. He argued that when humans long ago had lived in an isolated state of nature they had been perfectly content and happy, like God. It was only when they began to have to have contact with other people that problems came. Rousseau recognised that it was impossible to return to the blissful isolation of a pre-society existence, but he recommended that people should cut themselves off as much as they could from relationships with other members of society. In particular he wanted to abolish the family. This would leave only self-absorbed individuals and the State.

THE EFFECT ON HUMANISM AND THE EFFECT OF HUMANISM

The Renaissance humanist emphasis on classical education, the Reformation emphasis on the individual, and the Enlightenment emphasis on reason – all good things in themselves – combined to set the stage for a rejection of traditional Christian beliefs.

Some people argued, even before the eighteenth century, that God and the supernatural could not be proved by science or deduced by reason, and therefore they did not exist. Those who still believed in God began to be seen as foolish and uneducated.

As faith became more personal and individualistic, some Christians created their own interpretations of Christianity and scripture, so as to have the type of faith that suited them best. Elements of Christianity and scripture that did not fit with their lifestyle, worldview or theology were discarded.

Although concepts such as tolerance and human rights largely owe their origins to the Christian understanding that all people are equally worthy of respect and dignity because they are made in the image of God, humanists developed these ideas further. They applied them in various societies to areas like culture, race, gender and politics, doing much good in helping to establish human rights, gender equality, freedom of speech and freedom of religion.

But in some places the concept of tolerance is now used to justify or promote any type of behaviour, practice or belief. Frank Furedi (2011) states that tolerance has become a refusal to make any judgement at all. Where there are no absolute rights and wrongs, the principle of tolerance means that things which were seen as immoral and unethical just a few years ago are widely accepted and sometimes even celebrated. Christians who oppose such practices are labelled intolerant. It is ironic that some societies will tolerate any view point or behaviour except the views of Christians who challenge injustice, immorality and unrighteousness; in these situations tolerance has become intolerance.

Over-tolerance has also crept into parts of the Church, where Christians have become hesitant to preach the Gospel or to stand up for issues of righteousness and justice for fear of being labelled intolerant. Some Christians even support behaviour and beliefs that are contrary to traditional interpretations of the Bible. Same-sex relationships, euthanasia and abortion are just a few examples.

The separation of state and Church is supported by many Christians as well as by humanists. But most Christians believe that, despite such a separation, Christians should be able to advise, guide and hold the state accountable as well as express their faith within the public space. Humanists, on the other hand, are working to remove religion from the public space and preferably from the private sphere as well. The new civic religion, which is gaining increasing power within many Western state structures, is seeking to undermine and dilute the influence of Christianity on society.

3
RECENT HISTORY OF HUMANISM

THE LONG NINETEENTH CENTURY 1789-1914

Much happened in the relatively short period between the end of the Age of Enlightenment and the start of the First World War. This period is often referred to as the Long Nineteenth Century. The last part of the eighteenth century was a time of great scientific discovery and progress increased even more rapidly in the nineteenth century. It was a period when reason and intellect were held in high regard. Education, based on the Greek and Roman *studia humanitas*, became even more widespread. This form of education promoted questioning and scepticism. It tended to make people more politically and socially active.

Modern democracy has its origins in theological debates in the seventeenth century about the implications of all people being equally created in the image of God and the limits set by Scripture to the authority of kings. In the long nineteenth century, those who followed humanist thinking developed these ideas further and started discussing the idea of a perfect world or

Utopia. The questioning attitude, the ideals of democracy and pursuit of an ideal society led to a number of revolutions or wars for independence, such as the French Revolution (1789-1799).

The Industrial Revolution and Poor Working Conditions
Advances in science led to the Industrial Revolution. The rural poor moved to the cities to find work in the new factories but working conditions were often dreadful. Men, women and children were required to work long hours, with few rests, for low pay, in extremely dangerous and unhealthy conditions.

The Creation of Civic Institutions
Numerous ethical and charitable societies and other civic institutions emerged in the Americas and Europe promoting the human rights of these workers and other marginalised groups in society.

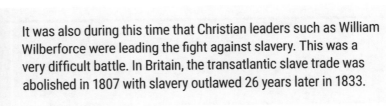

It was also during this time that Christian leaders such as William Wilberforce were leading the fight against slavery. This was a very difficult battle. In Britain, the transatlantic slave trade was abolished in 1807 with slavery outlawed 26 years later in 1833.

Many of these societies were Christian but, particularly in the second half of the nineteenth century, an increasing number were atheist and humanist. Humanist thinkers at the time believed that morality, ethics and human rights could exist in the absence of religion. In fact some believed that religion promoted helplessness, was evil and was one of the areas which should be fought against to free people. Much of this thinking was influenced by the rise of socialism and Marxism.

The Rise of Marxism
Karl Marx (1818-1883), a German activist, believed that religion resulted in oppression and produced an unjust and inhumane society. He is famous for saying "Religion is the sigh of the oppressed creature, the heart of a heartless world, and the soul of soulless conditions. It is the opium of the people." His reasoning was that religion, and Christianity in particular, took

people's focus off the needs, realities and wrongs of the time. He believed that because people placed their faith and hope in a future salvation or a better place called heaven, they did little to resist and fight the injustices of the present. Marx thought that if people were freed from their belief in God, then injustice would end. He believed that there was no higher being than humankind and that religion must be overthrown. He said, "To abolish religion as the illusory happiness of the people is to demand their real happiness." Marx did not believe that people had any "inward nature" or could reason or had the freewill to make choices. This makes democracy meaningless and leaves one-party forcible government as the only logical option. It could be said that his humanist beliefs actually took away the human nature of people.

Marx's views did much to promote the humanist mandate to criticise, attack and abolish all forms of Christianity and religion in society which is so widespread today.

"Human communities desire to make the world a better place. The desire for Utopia has a long history and the emergence of human rights is linked to the history of utopianism.

"Utopic visions of society like revolutionary communism and reformed capitalism have collapsed and human rights is the only form of utopianism that exists today. It occupies the space left open by the departure of alternative visions of transforming societies."

Vinay Samuel (2016)

Darwin and *On the Origin of Species*
Marxism was not the only movement in the nineteenth century that was challenging belief in God. One of the most influential events in the development of the humanist movement was the publication of Charles Darwin's book *On the Origin of Species* in 1859 which described how natural selection had gradually produced the different species of animals and plants. This was widely promoted by humanists as unquestionable proof that there was no creator God or purposefully ordered natural law.

It led to a crisis of faith for many people who became either atheists or agnostics. Science and religion became even more separate. The theory of evolution became the standard explanation for human existence and is widely taught in schools and universities today.

Thomas Henry Huxley (1826-1895), a great supporter of the work of Darwin, was the first person to use the term "agnostic". He was building on a long tradition of philosophical scepticism. Gradually the meaning of the word settled into the current sense of someone who does not know whether or not God exists, or someone who believes it is impossible to know whether or not God exists.

The Formalisation of Humanism

Humanism as a movement became more formalised in the second half of the nineteenth century. In 1860 the term "humanist" was used in print for the first time. In 1866 the National Secular Society was founded in Britain, one of the first humanist societies of its kind. Across the world similar humanist societies started emerging. In 1896 the various ethical societies in Britain came together to form the Union of Ethical Societies. This eventually became the British Humanist Association in 1967. Likewise, on the other side of the Atlantic Ocean, the American Ethical Union, established in 1886, went on to found the International Humanist and Ethical Union in 1952. Today, the International Humanist and Ethical Union is the umbrella organisation for the global humanist movement.

EARLY TWENTIETH CENTURY: HUMANISM WANES IN THE LIGHT OF WARS AND DEPRESSION

The Long Nineteenth Century ended with the First World War (1914-1918), one of the worst and most widespread wars the world had ever known. Although humanism was becoming much more formalised as a movement, support for and the spread of humanism slowed down in the time between the two world wars. The ideals of a Utopian society had been dashed by the realities and atrocities of the First World War. Governments became much more authoritarian. The Russian socialist and Marxist movements that resulted in the Russian revolution (1917) were replaced by the communist and, later, the Stalinist totalitarian regimes. In America the 1920s was a time of radical and political activism as well as economic prosperity. This changed after the stock market crash of 1929 and the Great Depression (1929-1939) that followed, bringing unemployment, poverty, hunger and enormous suffering. A more conservative lifestyle, where there was little questioning of authority, was promoted. The First World War had placed great economic pressure on Europe. The Great Depression affected Europe and added even more to its economic troubles.

Fascist governments started to emerge in countries such as Italy, Germany, Poland, Greece, Hungary, Romania and Yugoslavia, seeking to bring about economic reform. These governments rejected Marxism and international socialism, the core tenets of the humanist movement, and instead promoted national socialism, where the State controlled the infrastructure and resources of the country. Most Fascist governments were led by strong leaders or dictators. Famous Fascist leaders are Mussolini, who ruled Italy from 1922 to 1944, and Hitler, who ruled Nazi Germany from 1933 to 1945. All of these global factors and events made it very difficult for humanist ideas to spread easily during this time.

HUMANISM INTENSIFIES EFFORTS TO SPREAD

Despite, or perhaps because of, these setbacks humanists continued and renewed their efforts to promote their beliefs. Humanists blamed capitalism and greed for the economic collapse which resulted in the Great Depression. In 1933, two humanist scholars, Roy Wood Sellars and Raymond Bragg, published a document entitled *A Humanist Manifesto*. The document was signed by a number of notable scholars, politicians and thinkers of the time. It was strongly socialist and outlined the humanist stance and promoted humanism as a religion to replace that of Christianity.

One of the most significant results of the manifesto was the formalisation of humanist belief, its aims and objectives as a movement, and a call to action. Humanists at this time realised that, in order to survive and promote the humanist agenda, they needed to create strong and active organisational structures. A number of new humanist organisations began to be created in Europe and America in the late 1940s.

HUMANISM BEGINS TO THRIVE

Towards the end of the Second World War (1939-1945) and into the 1950s and 1960s humanist support began to grow. Most of Europe had been exposed to the horrors of war and had become aware of the evils of the Nazi concentration camps. Many people questioned the frailties of human nature and looked for morality and ethics to guide future human behaviour. At an international level, humanism also allowed for governments and societies, which were previously divided on religious and ethical grounds, to be united in common causes such as the development and protection of human rights. This paved the way for organisations such as the United Nations and the creation of human rights charters, many based on humanist beliefs.

The United Nations is a specific example of humanism at work. The first Director General of UNESCO, the UN organisation promoting education, science, and culture, was the 1962 Humanist of the Year Julian Huxley, who practically drafted UNESCO'S charter by himself. The first Director-General of the World Health Organisation was the 1959 Humanist of the Year Brock Chisholm. One of this organisation's greatest accomplishments has been the wiping of smallpox from the face of the earth. And the first Director-General of the Food and Agricultural Organisation was British Humanist John Boyd Orr.

http://americanhumanist.org/Humanism/What_is_Humanism

A Humanist Manifesto, later renamed the *Humanist Manifesto I*, was followed up by *Humanist Manifesto II* in 1973 and the *Humanist Manifesto III: a successor to the Humanist Manifesto of 1933*, published in 2003. All three documents will be examined in chapter 4.

PRESENT DAY

Humanism is stronger today than it has ever been, and is spreading fast. One of the growing movements within the world is that of New Atheism, which is being led by the British Humanist Association's patron, Richard Dawkins. Dawkins is best known for his book, *The God Delusion*.

> In *The God Delusion*, Dawkins rightly points out that religions have been responsible for violence, warfare and acts of cruelty not only in the past but also in the present. However, in the twentieth century (at least) by far the greatest number of unnecessary deaths were caused by atheist humanist regimes, most of the casualties coming from the State's persecution of its own citizens.

Many humanists such as Dawkins and other New Atheists are aggressively spreading their beliefs. They are no longer simply trying to survive or passively promoting their belief system. They are actively attacking religions, and in particular Christianity. Worldwide campaigns, lobbying and legal actions are being targeted against supporters of religion. Humanist beliefs are firmly entrenched in most Western educational and legal systems. One effect of this is the decline of Christianity in Europe. Many people are humanists without even realising it. They may not belong to any humanist organisation or even recognise the term humanism, but because of their exposure to a humanist-based society and their humanist education, their belief system and worldview are significantly humanist.

A society immersed in a humanist ideology has influenced and impacted the Church. Not only has morality slipped within the Church, but also some parts of the Church are now taking an active role in promoting and propagating this humanist worldview within the Christian community and society at large. One small example of this is the growing use – in society at large and amongst Christians too – of the word "partner" instead of "husband" or "wife". Using this term hides whether the couple in question are married or unmarried, man and woman or same-sex, and sends the message that such differences are of no significance.

Return of Pelagianism

The belief that humans are inherently good has been one of the recurring heresies of the Church throughout the ages. In this, it accords with humanist ideas of the innate goodness of all human beings. The heresy is called Pelagianism, after a fifth century British monk called Pelagius.

Pelagius travelled to Rome and was shocked to find great immorality in that centre of Christendom. Hoping to encourage Christians to live better lives, he taught that human nature is essentially good and Christians can therefore choose to obey God and thus be saved. He rejected the Christian teaching on original sin and the doctrine that people can only be saved by God's grace because it is impossible for them to obey God perfectly.

Pelagianism has been condemned by more church councils than any other heresy in history; yet it persisted, especially in Britain and the countries which Britain influenced. This doctrine is shaping large sections of contemporary Christianity. Many Christians today prefer a religion without dogma and love without truth. According to Michael S. Horton, 77% of evangelical Christians in 1994 held this belief without realising it was a heresy.

> **"We cannot but decide that their [the Pelagians'] doctrine fails to recognise the misery of sin and evil, that in its deepest roots it is godless, that it knows, and seeks to know, nothing of redemption."**
>
> **Adolf von Harnack (1899)**

One implication of denying original sin and affirming the primacy of free will is the belief that we humans can be masters of our destiny and of the world. Another implication is the belief that our social structures do not need renewal and neither do human beings. The emphasis on love – without boundaries – can become an emphasis on fulfilling our selfish desires, so that pleasure becomes a goal in itself.

The Other Pelagius – the Martyr

Although the fifth century Pelagius was a British heretic, there was a tenth century Pelagius who was a Spanish martyr. His uncle, a bishop, was captured by the Muslims who ruled much of Spain at that time. The bishop persuaded Caliph Abdurrahman to do a prisoner exchange, letting the bishop go and holding instead ten-year-old Pelagius. Apparently the bishop had intended to send a ransom payment to free his nephew but this never happened. Pelagius, who was a remarkably handsome child, remained in prison in Córdoba for three years.

Then the Caliph asked to see the Christian boy prisoner. His good looks stunned the whole court. The Caliph offered to make Pelagius a page in the court if he would convert to Islam but Pelagius refused the offer, saying that he would obey the Caliph in everything "but first I am Christ's. Nothing may part me from Him." The Caliph was enraged and as Pelagius continued to affirm his faith in Christ, so the Caliph grew angrier. He was also, say the traditional accounts, moved by homosexual desire for the handsome 13-year-old but this too Pelagius resisted.

Eventually the Caliph ordered that Pelagius be hung up by his wrists until the pain forced him to deny Christ. But Pelagius remained faithful. The Caliph offered him the choice: "Happy freedom, honour, my favour and protection - or death. Choose!" The boy replied, "I have chosen: Christ!"

The Caliph had him torn to pieces with iron pincers, his hands and feet cut off, and finally thrown in the river.

Emerging Church

One area of concern to many Christians is the growth of a movement called the Emerging Church (or Emergent Church). This is not a formal denomination or organisation but rather a group of Christians, mainly young, who have similar worldviews on various issues, in particular on how to practise Christianity within a postmodern context. The intention of these Christians is good in that they are trying to make the Gospel message relevant to a humanist and unbelieving world, and they have a great concern to alleviate poverty and social deprivation. However, there are a number of things within the Emerging Church's way of practising Christianity which must be questioned.

The Emerging Church movement believes that Christianity and the Church have been too exclusive in the past, and that there may be other ways of discovering God and Jesus. They say that a person should be judged by what they do and not by their beliefs, quoting James 2:18. "But someone will say, 'You have faith and I have deeds.' Show me your faith without deeds, and I will show you my faith by what I do."

The Emerging Church

"They offer 'social justice', in the name of the reign and mission of God – a new friendly Christianity that welcomes doctrinal change, embraces diversity and seeks to right the wrongs in the structures of society. This call to 'join the revolution' appeals to young minds."

Joseph Boot (2014, p. 12)

They say that as long as a person is good and acts justly they can be considered a follower of Christ. They also believe that there may not be absolute truths and that Scripture can be interpreted in a number of different ways. Scripture is not seen as literal or in some cases as inspired by God. So parts of the Bible that do not fit in with the Emerging Church worldview are ignored or overlooked. Commandments are seen as guides rather than instructions to be obeyed.

Relationship with Other Religions

Another feature of the Church that has been impacted by humanism is its relationship with other religions and the drive towards a civic religion, mentioned in Chapter 1. Many Christian leaders have been active in promoting a civic religion. The Swiss theologian Hans Küng, who founded the World Ethos Institute at the University of Tübingen, is one such leader. Küng strongly supports interfaith dialogue, which he says is needed for the survival of the human race. In *Christianity: Essence, History, and Future* (1995) he says,

> No peace among the nations
> without peace among the religions.
> No peace among the religions
> without dialogue between the religions.
> No dialogue between the religions
> without investigation of the foundation of the religions.

He believes that there is truth in all religions and that a global ethical code can be found when the morals and values of religions are reduced to a common denominator. He also drafted "A Declaration Toward a Global Ethic" which was supported by a number of prominent Christian leaders as well as leaders from other religious groups. This Declaration has had a major influence in how the United Nations approaches religious differences and has been used to justify the promotion of civic religion by governments.

FAMOUS HUMANISTS

Richard Dawkins
Evolutionary biologist, author, and winner of Humanist of the Year 1996 and numerous other humanist awards

John Dewey
American philosopher, psychologist and educationalist, one of the first signatories of *A Humanist Manifesto*

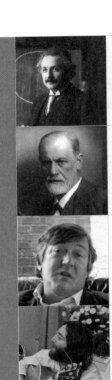

Albert Einstein
Mathematician, served on the board of the Humanist Society of New York

Sigmund Freud
Early founder of psychology and psychoanalysis

Stephen Fry
British actor and comedian

John Lennon
British musician and songwriter, member of the band The Beatles

Abraham Maslow
American psychologist, famous for Maslow's Hierarchy of Needs, was Humanist of the Year 1967

Salman Rushdie
Controversial author of *The Satanic Verses*, received an Outstanding Lifetime Achievement Award from the American Humanist Association

Steve Wozniak
Inventor and co-founder of Apple, received the Isaac Asimov Science award from the American Humanist Association in 2011

4
WHAT HUMANISTS BELIEVE

The Humanist Manifestos are a series of documents that outline the aims, objectives, values and beliefs of the humanist movement. The original document was written in 1933 and called *A Humanist Manifesto*. It was later renamed *Humanist Manifesto I*, so it could not be confused with later revisions as the document evolved. Although there are many revisions, most notably in 1973, *Humanist Manifesto II*, and in 2003, *Humanist Manifesto III*, all maintain the core tenets of humanism namely atheism, naturalism, evolution, moral relativism, celebration of humankind and the pursuit of a utopian world.

The core beliefs of humanism can be summarised as follows:

Atheism
Humanists do not believe in God. Instead they think that humans have invented or imagined the existence of God. They feel that any belief in a God or the creation of religions is dangerous to society and holds back the development of humans as a species.

Naturalism

Humanists believe that the natural world is all that exists. They therefore do not believe in God, the supernatural, a spiritual world, an afterlife, heaven or hell.

Evolution

Because humanists are atheists and naturalists, they do not believe that there is a creator. Instead they believe that all life was started by a natural event without the influence of a God. Organisms, including humans, have evolved over millions of years. Humans are the pinnacle of this evolutionary process. Creationism is seen as non-scientific. Humans are merely biological and as such do not have a soul or any spiritual component.

Moral and Ethical Relativism

Humanists do not believe that there are any moral absolutes or ethical standards. Morality depends on situations and each individual can and should decide what is right and wrong for them. People should not rely on any religious instruction or values. As there is no God humankind cannot be guided by Him; instead each person is encouraged to develop their own rules for living.

Celebration of Humankind

Humankind is celebrated as the highest being in existence. As God does not exist, humans should not call upon God to intervene in the world or in the lives of individuals. Seeking salvation is seen as a waste of energy and a distraction from attempting to solve the problems of the world. Having a hope of salvation is seen as making people apathetic about the problems of the day. Humanists argue that the survival of the human race is the responsibility of humans and it is up to each individual to do something because there are no messiahs or saviours in this world or the next.

What Humanists Say About Faith in God
From the Preface of Humanist Manifesto II

As in 1933, humanists still believe that traditional theism, especially faith in the prayer-hearing God, assumed to love and care for persons, to hear and understand their prayers, and to be able to do something about them, is an unproved and outmoded faith. Salvationism, based on mere affirmation, still appears as harmful, diverting people with false hopes of heaven hereafter. Reasonable minds look to other means for survival.

Utopia

Humanists are striving for a perfect world which is not divided by borders. Instead they promote a "socialised and cooperative economic order" (*Manifesto I*) and "a world order, based upon transnational federal government" (*Manifesto II*). All forms of religion must be removed from every part of society. This world order should be socialist, where resources are equally shared, capitalism is eradicated and where there are no travel restrictions.

HUMANIST MANIFESTO I (1933)

The first manifesto, written in 1933, set the tone of all the future versions that followed. The manifesto clearly describes humanism as a new religion which is to replace all other religions that believe in God and a creator. It goes on to state that the establishment of the humanist religion is necessary to reshape and change society. It describes itself as a "vital, fearless and frank religion" with a mandate to spread itself and challenge other religions. The manifesto is made up of 15 affirmations where the core tenets of this new belief system are formally presented for the first time.

HUMANIST MANIFESTO II (1973)

Humanist Manifesto II was developed by the American Humanist Association in 1973. It was originally signed by 282 prominent educationalists, scientists and government officials. Later many tens of thousands also signed. The world had changed significantly in the 40 years since the first manifesto. There had been a world war and communism, based on the humanist ideal of shared resources, had spread across the world resulting in millions of deaths. The second manifesto is made up of 17 points which affirm the core beliefs, expand upon some and deal with issues not mentioned in the first manifesto.

A rejection of God, creation and religion is even more strongly emphasised and encouraged. The separation of Church and State along with the removal of any religious ideology from public society are seen as imperative. The State should not support any religious activity, either directly or implicitly. The ideal of a single world order is also expanded upon.

The elimination of discrimination based on race, religion, sex, age or national origin is mentioned for the first time; so too are the subjects of war and the environment. Another new mention is sexuality. Religions are criticised for repressing sexual conduct. Rights to birth control, abortion and divorce are promoted. Any sexual expression and exploration between consenting adults is encouraged, as is sex education for children which teaches them sexual freedom and activity.

HUMANIST MANIFESTO III (2003)

Many of the principles of the humanists have been adopted by governments, intergovernmental organisations such as the United Nations, and international organisations. However, despite the efforts of humanists and these organisations to promote the humanist agenda, wars, poverty and suffering have increased. In 2003 the American Humanist Association released the *Humanist Manifesto III: a successor to the Humanist Manifesto of 1933*. This took numerous people three years to compile. It was extremely popular and signed by hundreds of prominent scientists and academics including 22 Nobel Prize winners.

Humanism is a broad term and there are many other philosophies and ideologies which have taken elements of humanism and incorporated them into their belief systems. This book mostly focuses on what is known as **Modern Humanism**, or simply **Humanism**, but there are other types of humanism. Below are three of the most common.

Secular Humanism. This is a branch of Modern Humanism but with an even stronger focus on removing all religion and God from society.

Religious Humanism. Religious humanists practise humanism as a religion. They meet regularly and hold humanist rituals. They have ordained leaders who perform humanist ceremonies such as weddings and funerals. Some religious humanists believe in God. Some are universalists, believing that there are many ways to God.

Christian Humanism. These humanists believe in God and Jesus but still hold many of the other doctrines of humanism such as celebration of humankind and ethical relativism (there are no absolute rights or wrongs). Christian humanists can be typically divided into two schools of thought: they may believe that God is distant and it is up to each person and humankind as a whole to look after themselves; or they believe in a form of grace that allows people to do whatever they want and that there are no consequences because God will forgive them (sometimes called hyper-grace, as described in chapter 1).

The 2003 manifesto is not arranged as a list of affirmations, as was the case in the previous two documents. Instead it consists of a number of short paragraphs or beliefs. The language and tone of the third manifesto is less aggressive and more subtle. However, the document still holds on to the core humanist principles that were outlined in the first two manifestos. One very distinct difference from the first two manifestos is the mention of humanism as a philosophy or worldview. The term religion is no longer used. This is a very intentional and important omission.

Humanists have been extremely successful in removing religion from society, especially from public spaces such as schools, universities and government institutions. While Christianity and the ability to worship freely have been attacked by humanism, a humanist belief system has been widely accepted within these same institutions.

Recently humanists have been taking care to avoid humanism being labelled as a religion. Their concern is that their beliefs would also have to be excluded from public spaces on the same religious grounds which they have used to attack other belief systems.

IS HUMANISM A RELIGION?

In the first manifesto humanists describe themselves as a religious movement but most humanist organisations have since distanced themselves from being categorised as a religion. Instead they state that there is a small element of Religious Humanists who practise humanism as an alternative religion. Humanists who distance themselves from the term religion say they are secular humanists, modern humanists or just plain humanists.

Oliver L Reiser, signatory of the first Manifesto wrote in the journal _The Humanist:_

"The one great hope for democracy lies in the development of a non-supernaturalistic religion which, unlike other intellectual movements, will be non-academic in its appeal to all civilized individuals. This new foundation for a coming world-order must be the emergent outcome of the thought-content of a universalized culture. . .

"The god of this coming world-religion, that is, the object of reverence of scientific humanism, is the spirit of humanity in its upward striving."

Some humanists argue that religion is the belief in, worship of or devotion to a supernatural being or realm. They say that because they do not believe in the supernatural they cannot be considered a religion, and describe their beliefs instead as a worldview, ideology or philosophy.

A Secular Humanist Declaration was written in 1980 as a response to the heavy criticism which the movement, and in particular the *Humanist Manifesto II*, had received from some Christian groups. The Christians had suggested that humanism should be called a religious movement. The *Declaration* countered this accusation by saying, "Secular humanism expressed a set of moral values and a nontheistic philosophical and scientific viewpoint that could not be equated with religious faith."

Court rulings: In America there have been a number of court rulings that have classified humanism as a religion.

Torcasco v Watkins (1961): "Among religions in this country which do not teach what would generally be considered a belief in the existence of God are Buddhism, Taoism, Ethical Culture, Secular Humanism, and others."

US v Segeer (1965) allowed humanists to avoid being called up to fight in the Vietnam War on religious grounds.

Smith v Board of School Commissioners of Mobile County (1987). The judge in this case produced a 172-page report which concluded that secular humanism is a religion: "For purposes of the First Amendment, secular humanism is a religious belief system, entitled to the protections of, and subject to the prohibitions of, the religious clauses."

Washington Ethical Society v District of Columbia (1957) was awarded tax emption status based on religious grounds. This allowed other humanist organisations who deny they are religious to be tax exempt as well.

A movement that does not believe in a god or the supernatural can still be a religion. There are many non-theistic religions such as Buddhism and Taoism which do not believe in a god. Even if a movement calls itself "secular" it could still be considered a religion. The humanist movement demonstrates some distinct elements that categorise it as a religion: it has a set of beliefs regarding humanity and the existence of the universe, it has a core set of defined values, it has organisational structures, and it systematically works to expand, promote and spread its belief system. Its belief system is also exclusive; just as someone cannot be both a Christian and a Muslim, humanists believe that someone cannot be a humanist and a Christian or a humanist and a Muslim.

Enchantment

Some atheists and agnostics have pointed out that their secularist beliefs lack what has been called by Bishop Richard Harries (2008) the "enchantment" of religion. Some have recommended that atheists and secularists should try to capture this enchantment by copying what they consider best in the practices of religion, but of course without believing in God. The atheist philosopher Alain de Botton (2012) suggests that atheists could find inspiration, consolation in suffering, and many other good things from "a selective reverence for religious rituals and concepts" and suggests building temples to atheism. Charles Moore (2012) has countered this by pointing out that the things which de Botton finds useful in religion depend on the religion being true.

HUMANIST RELIGION BEING IMPOSED UPON SOCIETY

The question of whether humanism is a religion is a very important consideration for humanism is increasingly the basis of most educational systems, textbooks, psychological theory, societal norms and values and sexual behaviour, as well as new national and international laws. If humanism is a religion then governments, intergovernmental organisations, educational institutions are propagating, supporting and imposing religious values on many people who do not support such beliefs. Many Christians are being forcibly exposed to the humanist belief system which they are opposed to. Surely humanism must also be excluded from the public space on religious grounds, or at least Christians and followers of other religions should have the option of enjoying the same rights that humanists enjoy within society.

5
THE HUMANIST AGENDA

Humanism aims to replace Christian morality with a civic and worldly way of living which is against the will and instruction of God. The Bible is very clear that God will judge a society that has turned morality on its head:

> Woe to those who call evil good
>   and good evil,
> who put darkness for light
>   and light for darkness,
> who put bitter for sweet
>   and sweet for bitter.
>   Isaiah 5:20

The humanist agenda is laid out clearly in the humanist manifestos, declarations and organisational constitutions. It is summarised well by the International Humanist and Ethical Union. The IHEU is an international organisation that represents the global humanist movement, with 116 member organisations from over 50 countries.

VISION AND MISSION

The vision of IHEU is a humanist and secular world; a world in which human rights are respected and everyone is able to live a life of dignity.

The mission of IHEU is to build and represent a humanism worldwide that defends human rights and promotes humanist values.

STRATEGY

The long term strategic aims of IHEU are:

to **promote** humanism as a non-theistic life stance throughout the world

to **represent** humanists within the international community

to **defend** human rights and the rights of humanists

to **develop** organised humanism in every part of the world

to **build** a strong and effective global organisation

The humanist aim is to make the world secular and to replace all other religions with humanism. Humanism has already spread across large sections the world, influencing schools, media, government and international organisations. Recently humanism has become even more proactive in its approach. A good example of this is an extract from the *American Humanist Association Strategic Plan 2007*:

The American Humanist Association seeks to foster a profound change in American culture, promoting a society more strongly aligned with Humanist values and displacing the Influence of religious fundamentalism and dogma. One of the principle means to accomplish this goal is by working to increase public awareness and acceptance of Humanism. The propagation of Humanism in America is not just another organizational goal but a mission that can serve the larger interests of the nation and the global community. A substantial increase in public understanding and acceptance of Humanism will establish a needed counterweight to fundamentalist religious beliefs and practices, and will pave the way toward the evolution of a more humane and rational society.

This agenda is not limited to the Western world; humanist organisations elsewhere are equally open regarding their aims and objectives:

"Humanism believes in the development of ethics on a non-theistic basis in which human beings are considered to be free and responsible without referring to powers considered to be of higher importance than human beings themselves." - *Indian Humanist Union*

"To promote the separation of church and state and foster the development of reason, compassion and critical thinking for all Kenyans through secular education and community support" - *Mission Statement of Kenyan Humanist Association*

"Questioning religious dogma and its relationship to discourses of human rights and to facilitate collaboration among those in support of humanist ideals and interested in the advancement of a secular Jamaica" – *Jamaica Secular Humanist Society*

"It promotes secular humanism as a progressive philosophy suggesting that human beings, given the right education, can be ethical and morally upright even without divine interference." – *Humanist Alliance Philippines*

STAGES OF HUMANISM EXPANSION

Humanists use well established and successful methods to introduce the humanist agenda into society. One such method includes the following stages:

Stage One: Tolerance. Humanists first urge society to tolerate or accept a humanist idea, value, belief, ideology or behaviour that would be largely seen as contrary to cultural norms, values or religious beliefs, especially those of Christianity. This is done through popular media, advocacy, legal action, media campaigns, demonstrations and appeals to governments and international bodies.

> The British humanist Richard Dawkins (1976), reflecting on how ideas spread and evolve to effect cultural and social change, coined the term "meme". He shortened *mimeme*, the Greek for imitation, to create a word for an idea, behaviour or style that is spread from one person to another. He also wanted it to sound similar to the word "gene" as his suggestion was that memes spread through a population in a similar way to genes. Memes are passed on through writing, speech, gestures, images or any other media that is able to be copied or mimicked easily. Memes are often spread across social media and have an ability to "go viral", becoming very popular and circulating quickly from person to person.

Stage Two: Equality. Humanists then put pressure on authorities and society to recognise these humanist beliefs or behaviours and place them on an equal level with those of the current society or Christianity.

Stage Three: Reversal of norms. Humanists then work to make the previous norms and values of society and Christianity seem abnormal, silly, backward, evil or a threat to human progress. Humanists would argue that previous norms and values are restrictive and conflict with human rights. Christians are often labelled as irrational, unreasonable, prejudiced fundamentalists for holding on to their beliefs and values.

Stage Four: Aggressive action. The fourth and final stage is an effort to make the previous norms and Christian values illegal by bringing legal action against groups who uphold these values and beliefs. Christian groups have found themselves having to defend values and beliefs that were previously widely accepted or even celebrated within society.

Areas where humanists are particularly active include education, the media, popular culture, governments, international governing bodies, and legal action.

EDUCATION

"I am convinced that the battle for humankind's future must be waged and won in the public school classroom by teachers who correctly perceive their role as the proselytizers of a new faith: a religion of humanity that recognizes and respects the spark of what theologians call divinity in every human being.

"These teachers must embody the same selfless dedication as the most rabid fundamentalist preachers, for they will be ministers of another sort, utilizing a classroom instead of a pulpit to convey humanist values in whatever subject they teach, regardless of the educational level – the preschool, day care or large state university.

"The classroom must and will become an arena of conflict between the old and the new – the rotting corpse of Christianity, together with all its adjacent evils and misery, and the new faith of humanism, resplendent in its promise of a world in which the never-realised Christian ideal of 'love thy neighbour' will finally be achieved."

John Dunphy, *The Humanist* (Jan/Feb 1983, p. 26)

Perhaps the most influential and lasting effect humanism has had on society has been in education. The main factor here was the belief that everything should be explained through reason, logic and science.

God as creator, or even the existence of God, could not be explained by science and so a growing movement of academic atheists emerged. They began to influence what was taught and believed about God, creation, the role of the Church, liberalism and tolerance. This movement had an effect on education that is still felt in many Western-based school systems today. It has gone a long way in shaping how people view the world now.

This is further strengthened by the acceptance of educational and psychological theories which were developed by many prominent humanists including the likes of Abraham Maslow, Carl Rodger, John Dewey, B.F. Skinner and Benjamin Spock. Almost all modern educational methodology has been influenced by these humanist educators.

Using education to spread humanism is seen as vital to the humanist cause. Many of the original signatories of the various humanist manifestos and declarations were educationalists - more than a third of the 34 original signatories of the *Humanist Manifesto I*; and 33 of the 58 signatories of *The Secular Humanist Declaration*. Humanists have influenced not just *what* is being taught in schools, colleges and universities but *how* it is taught, affecting generations of people and moulding a humanist worldview and culture. Opportunities to "teach virtue" are being squeezed out.

A prominent American humanist wrote:

> In considering the influence of humanism on education I thought it might be useful to go through the Humanist Manifesto II and check all the ideas expressed there which I felt had been taught to me when I attended the public schools in my youth. The exercise turned out to be a very pleasant surprise to me. I had expected to check only six, eight, or perhaps 12 at the most; but when I had finished, I found that I had checked no less than 58 ideas. I had not fully appreciated just how much humanism had influenced modern education until I did this exercise.

> Richard Layton (1997)

MEDIA

Humanists are now making greater use of media to promote and spread humanism and its ideas. For example, in 2009 the British Humanist Association launched a major media campaign using advertisements on buses. Humanist slogans such as "There's probably no God. Now stop worrying and enjoy your life" appeared on thousands of buses and billboards across the country. The campaign was followed up by numerous other media initiatives across the UK, most notably the "Don't Label Me" campaign, which specifically targeted children and schools. The campaign implied it was bad for parents to bring up a child within a religious household and children should not be influenced by any form of religion within their homes.

This bus campaign was taken up by other humanist organisations across the world including Brazil, the USA, Australia, Canada, New Zealand, Finland, Germany, Ireland, Italy, the Netherlands, Spain, Sweden and Russia. Some of the slogans included: "The bad news is that God does not exist. The good news is that you do not need him" (Italy); "Atheism – celebrate reason" (Brazil and Australia); "Extraordinary claims require extraordinary evidence: Allah, bigfoot, UFOs; Homeopathy, Zeus, Psychics and Christ" (Canada); "Why believe in God? Just be good for goodness sake" (USA).

POPULAR CULTURE

Another way humanists influence popular culture and worldviews is through the television and movie industries. Television and films have a significant impact on belief systems and culture.

Secularist Bias at the BBC

The secular British periodical *The Spectator* has drawn attention to the fact that, in the words of Rupert Shortt (2016), "when secular humanists attack Christianity, they often fail to realise that it is the gospels which provide unseen elements in their own outlook." *The Spectator* continues "... there is a strong secularist bias our culture. It's an institutional bias that media folk, especially those at the BBC, aren't really aware of having: they think they're being neutral when they marginalise the 'divisive' topic of religion, and decide to commission yet another radio series about feminism or science or classics or whatever. They don't notice that they are subtly consigning Christian voices to the margins. The exclusion works like this. Everything non-religious is seen as a harmlessly neutral topic. It might or might not be your thing, but it's a valid part of our culture that deserves airtime. Religion, on the other hand, is seen as problematically contentious. It can only be talked about in a sombre anxious way. If Christianity has to be talked about, there must be great awareness that atheists and those of other faiths are likely to be a bit miffed. And so it's safer to avoid it, whenever possible, and stick to what is inoffensively neutral." Theo Hobson (2016)

Christianity and Christian values have, over the past few decades, become increasingly eroded, side-lined or criticised in popular media. This has been done subtly by portraying certain behaviours first as acceptable and then as desirable, for example, premarital sex, drug use and violence. More recently, television shows and movies have become more upfront in promoting humanism and humanist ideas, especially about the existence of God and the depiction of Christianity. Christians are often shown as judgemental, ignorant or extremist. Some humanist organisations even go as far as to recommend which television shows and movies have been written from a humanist perspective. These lists are substantial but include the likes of The Big Bang Theory, The West Wing, The Good Wife, The Mentalist, The Office, Star Trek, Bones, and House MD.

GOVERNMENTS AND INTERNATIONAL GOVERNING BODIES

Most national and regional humanist organisations are active in shaping country laws. Humanists place pressure on governments by demonstrations, lobbying, legal action, and media campaigns to remove religion, particularly Christianity, from public spaces, while at the same time replacing it with humanist ideas. By claiming to be non-religious, humanists enable their own beliefs to be accepted and promoted within public spaces. In some countries humanist organisations or individuals sit on advisory boards or working groups within government and directly influence the legal policies of countries.

Natural Law and Legal Positivism

"In modern jurisprudence, natural law is usually seen as contrasting with another approach within legal theory called 'legal positivism'. Legal positivism holds that there is no necessary connection between law and morality...Legal positivism which sets morality to one side, may be seen as the quintessential liberal legal theory. By contrast, natural law theory holds that law can only be understood as a moral phenomenon and that there is some necessary connection between law and morality."

Jonathan Burnside (2011) Professor of Law at Bristol University

How Humanists Managed to Separate Law from Morality
"The social changes were rarely argued through with clarity, or indeed honesty ... Despite endless public debates the abortion reformers entirely played down the significance of psychological health as a reason for a termination, passionately arguing that the bill was not a charter for abortion on demand – which it certainly became. The use of separation as ground for divorce, rather than proof of adultery, was said to be a measure that would strengthen marriage; if so, it was clearly a failure. It was argued and assumed that the end of hanging would not increase the rate of murder or violent crime. Both would soon rise sharply.

All these measures had the backing of small and dedicated campaigns, generally only a few thousand strong. Each depended on celebrity intellectuals of one kind or another, to finally slaughter legislation which went back to Victorian times ... "

Andrew Marr (2007) Political Editor of BBC News

This is not limited to national governments. Many prominent United Nations leaders are openly humanist. The IHEU, which tries to promote humanist agendas on global laws, resolutions and policies, has special consultative status with the United Nations. It has representation on the Human Rights Council and the Committee on the Rights of the Child. It also has general consultative status at UNICEF (United Nations Children's Emergency Fund). Of particular concern is the influence on global education policy through its advisory and operational work with UNESCO (United Nations Educational, Scientific and Cultural Organisation). In addition the IHEU acts as a consultant to the Council of Europe, and to the African Commission on Human and People's Rights.

LEGAL ACTION

Through the support of national humanist bodies and the IHEU, humanists have been using legal procedures or legal threats to attack Christianity and promote humanism. Humanists promote tolerance but are often intolerant themselves of any belief system or view point that is not humanist. Religious freedom, including the right to worship and express beliefs openly while upholding religious values, is often attacked by humanists, who state that such rights are against human rights. The American Humanist Association is probably the most active in this regard, filing hundreds of threatening letters and initiating numerous lawsuits annually. However, this trend is being vigorously replicated around the world.

Separation of Church and State

The relationship between Church and State has been a cause of much discussion and dissent over the centuries. The early Church existed as totally separate from the State. But the fourth century saw State and Church united (though their functions kept distinct) to form Christendom (meaning the "one Church, one State" system in which governments upheld and even enforced Christianity – see chapter 11).

Before, during and after the Reformation the struggle between Church and State took several forms. One was for complete separation, as supported by the Baptists and Anabaptists, another was for Church and State to be totally unified, and the third was to see them as overlapping. For those countries where the Church became a state religion, for example in Lutheran and Anglican countries after the Reformation, as time passed the influence of the state and its effects on the Church diminished. But a relationship still exists, whether in the form of monetary benefits, political influence, or a visible presence of each in the culture of the other.

The question that is now growing is whether that link should be cut. This would lead to the American system of a total separation between Church and State, but with the Church still influencing the state through its moral teaching and through Christian individuals involved in the political scene. Whilst the author of this book is sympathetic to the benefits of a link between Church and State, for theological reasons he believes that the Church should not be a formal part of the state.

In South Africa, in 2014, six schools had High Court proceedings initiated against them by a humanist organisation seeking to remove Christianity from the schools. The majority of the schools' parents and the majority of the governing bodies were in favour of a Christian ethos. However, the humanist organisation, which is not affiliated to the schools in any way, argued that because the schools received some state funding no religious activities could be allowed on school premises. As of March 2016 the case had not yet been decided.

Time-line of Development of "Hate Speech" Law in the UK

KEY

	Attempts to introduce laws
	Actual laws
	Prosecutions

1838

Blasphemy was a common law offence but since 1838 the law only protected beliefs held by the established church.

1977

Last prosecution under blasphemy law. James Kirkup and Gay News convicted after publication of Kirkup's poem that imagined a Roman soldier fantasising about having gay sex with the body of Jesus.

1983

The Law Commission reviewed the *1936 Public Order Act* which prohibited "threatening, abusive or insulting words" where they were likely to lead to a breach of the peace. As a result a new Public Order Act was passed in 1986, but its section 5 had not been recommended by the Law Commission.

1986

1986 Public Order Act section 5 made it an offence to say or display "threatening, abusive or insulting words" or display them within the hearing or sight of someone likely to be caused "distress" by them.

2001

Attempt to introduce an offence of "incitement to religious hatred" in the *Anti-terrorism, Crime and Security Bill* – but twice defeated in House of Lords.

2002

Pensioner Harry Smith was convicted under the *1986 Public Order Act* for carrying a placard around Bournemouth saying "stop immorality, stop homosexuality, stop lesbianism". In 2004 his appeal was rejected, although by then he had died.

2004

Attempt to introduce an offence of "incitement to religious hatred" into the *Serious Organised Crime and Police Bill* – failed due to lack of time.

2005-06

The government's original proposal for an incitement to religious hatred law was to criminalise any speech or written material that could be deemed to be "threatening, abusive or insulting" by anyone who heard or read them – regardless of whether or not that was the intention of the speaker or writer. The penalty was a maximum 7-year sentence or fine or both. The proposal did not apply to words said inside a private home, but would have applied to church sermons.

Racial and Religious Hatred Bill re-introduced the offence. However, MPs defied the government by backing House of Lords amendments that dramatically narrowed the scope of the law by limiting it to "threatening" words and introduced a broad protection for free speech that allowed "discussion, criticism or expressions of antipathy, dislike, ridicule, insult or abuse of particular religions or the beliefs or practices of their adherents, or of any other belief system or the beliefs or practices of its adherents, or proselytising or urging adherents of a different religion or belief system to cease practising their religion or belief system".

2008

Blasphemy law abolished by *2008 Criminal Justice and Immigration Act* section 79.

Criminal Justice and Immigration Bill. The Government attempted to introduce an incitement to homophobic hatred clause based on the incitement to religious hatred law, but with no free speech clause and a maximum 7-year prison sentence.

Criminal Justice and Immigration Bill. A cross-party free speech clause was introduced in the House of Lords stating: "Protection of freedom of expression (sexual orientation). In this Part, for the avoidance of doubt, the discussion or criticism of sexual conduct or practices or the urging of persons to refrain from or modify such conduct or practices shall not be taken of itself to be threatening or intended to stir up hatred." The government was forced by parliament to accept this.

2009

A Christian couple, Ben and Sharon Vogelenzang, who owned a hotel in Liverpool, were prosecuted following a dispute with a Muslim guest, before the judge threw out the case. However, the publicity during the nine months run-up to the court case destroyed their business.

2009 Coroners and Justice Bill. The government used this to try to remove the free speech clause in the 2008 Act claiming that the clause was "unnecessary". Their attempt was passed by the House of Commons but twice defeated in the House of Lords – meaning the government could then only have forced it through by the rare procedure of waiting a year and then using the Parliament Act.

2010

Street preacher Dale Mcalpine was arrested and detained for answering a question about his views on sexual ethics from a police community support officer after being overheard answering a passerby's question of by mentioning a number of "sins" referred to in the Bible, including blasphemy, drunkenness, fornication and same-sex relationships.

Prime Minister Gordon Brown said the government would use the Parliament Act to force through removal of the free speech clause in the *Coroners and Justice Bill*. However, his party were defeated in the 2010 election before it could do so.

2013

2013 Crime and Courts Act section 57 repeals section 5 of the 1986 Public Order Act as a result of a campaign by Christian organisations, secularists, comedians and human rights campaigners. This cross party amendment was initially resisted by the government.

2015-16

Northern Ireland Pastor James McConnell made statements in a sermon that were perceived as derogatory to Islam, was prosecuted under the 2003 Communications Act after the sermon was made available online. The judge finding him not guilty commented: "It is not the task of the criminal law to censor offensive utterances."

Time-line of Development of Humanist-Based Laws in the UK

KEY

	Government announcements
■	Humanist-based laws

1957

The Wolfenden Committee report recommended the decriminalisation of private homosexual activity between consenting adults over the age of 21, but with heavier penalties against homosexual activity in public places.

1967

Sexual Offences Act. A government-sponsored law implemented the recommendations of the Wolfenden Committee, legalising homosexual acts in private between men over 21. The law only applied to England and Wales.

Abortion Act. Extended the permitted reasons for an abortion from just the mother's life being at risk (which had been allowed since 1929) to risk to the mother's physical or mental health, risk that the child would be born seriously disabled, or risk to the mental health of the mother's children. It was claimed this would end the estimated 10,000 backstreet abortion occurring annually. In fact abortions increased to 180,000 a year with only 2% due to risk to the mother's physical health.

1969

Divorce Reform Act. Allowed "non-fault" divorce after a period of separation. It was claimed this would strengthen marriage. In fact, the divorce rate rose from around 7% of marriages to nearly 50% now.

1980

Scottish Criminal Justice Act decriminalised homosexual acts between men.

1982

Homosexual Offences (Northern Ireland) Order. Legalised homosexual acts between consenting adults (as a result of a ruling of the European Court of Human Rights).

1994

Criminal Justice and Public Order Act. Lowered the age of consent for homosexual acts to 18

1998

The government issued a consultation paper *Supporting Families* which described marriage as "the surest foundation for raising children".

2001

Lowered the age of consent for homosexual acts to 16.

2002

Adoption and Children Act. Allowed unmarried and same-sex couples to adopt children (came into force 2005). This was done despite the evidence that cohabiting couples were six times more likely to separate before their child's fifth birthday than married couples and no evidence showing same-sex couples adopting would be beneficial to children. It was claimed these provisions would widen the pool of adoptive parents. In fact, in combination with the 2007 Sexual Orientation Regulations, it led to the closure

The government agreed "not to reopen the debate on the subject of marriage and family structure".

The government withdrew funding for National Marriage Week. The government consultation report *Moving Forward Together* rephrased the government's 1998 commitment to marriage saying "the adult couple relationship is the cornerstone of the family". This paved the way for the Civil Partnerships Act 2004 and adoption by same-sex couples.

2003

Repeal of Section 28 of the 1988 Local Government Act which prohibited schools from "the teaching of the acceptability of homosexuality as a pretended family relationship".

2004

Civil Partnerships Act. Allowed a "civil partnership" between same-sex couples, defined in the law as a legally registered relationship between two people of the same sex.

2005

The Adoption and Children Act (2002) came into force allowing unmarried and same-sex couples to adopt children.

2007

Equality Act (Sexual Orientation) Regulations . Adoption agencies were prohibited from refusing to place children with same-sex couples. (This led directly to the closure of a number of Catholic adoption agencies which had been some of the most successful agencies at getting "hard to place" children adopted. Those providing bed and breakfast accommodation, including in their own homes, were prohibited from refusing to take same-sex couples. This led to some Christian B&B owners being specifically targeted by gay rights activists seeking to force them to rent a double room to them.

A judge in an employment tribunal overturned the "religious exemption" in the Employment Equality (Sexual Orientation) Regulations 2003, fining the Bishop of Hereford £47,000 for refusing to hire a homosexual youth worker on the grounds that his lifestyle was incompatible with Christian ethics.

2013

Marriage (Same Sex Couples) Act. Redefined marriage as no longer being between a man and a woman. The government consultation only asked *how* this change should be made, and disallowed any responses which said it should not happen at all.

6
HUMANISM, CHRISTIANITY AND SCIENCE

WHAT HUMANISTS BELIEVE ABOUT SCIENCE

Humanists believe that everything can and should be explained by science, reason and rational thought. They do not believe that there is any proof that God or the supernatural exists. Therefore they do not believe in a creator God. Instead they say that the "universe is self-existing and not created", and that "man is part of nature" and is a result of a continuous evolutionary process (*A Humanist Manifesto I*). Thus, life began without the intervention of God. *The Secular Humanist Declaration (1980)* goes further by stating that a belief in creation "may seriously undermine the credibility of science itself". This implies that criticism directed at humanist beliefs is not only a challenge to humanism but also a challenge to science and truth.

Humanists assume that Christianity is not compatible with science and that scientists cannot be Christians. Humanists feel that no rational, reasonable scientist could have a belief in God. The American Humanist Association states that humanism was formed by science. In other words, with all the acquired knowledge that science brings there is no reasonable option but to hold a humanist worldview. The humanist *Amsterdam Declaration 2002* takes an even stronger approach and states that science was actually created by humanism: "Humanism is the outcome of a long tradition of free thought that has inspired many of the world's great thinkers and creative artists and gave rise to science itself."

ARE CHRISTIANITY AND SCIENCE IN OPPOSITION TO EACH OTHER?

Humanists claim that they alone can be true scientists as scientific study requires an atheistic worldview. They also state that Christianity is against scientific progress, and that Christianity and science are in conflict with each other. However, the truth is that most Christians are very much in favour of scientific progress and discovery.

The Church has a long history of supporting scientific development. Up until the nineteenth century, including the time of the Renaissance and Enlightenment, the Roman Catholic Church was the leading financial sponsor of scientific research. In the seventeenth century the Jesuit order published more scientific papers than any other academic institution in the world. Cathedrals were sometimes designed with dual functions – places of worship and astronomical observatories.

The Basilica of St. Mary of the Angels and the Martyrs, Rome, was used as an observatory to track the movements of the sun and stars

Some of the top scientists in history were Christian. In fact before the nineteenth century, most scientists studied the natural world in order to discover more of God. With the advent of the industrial revolution scientific progress meant financial advancement and so new reasons for studying science emerged. Towards the end of the Enlightenment, humanists, such as Voltaire, a French philosopher and activist, began to accuse the Church and clergy of holding back scientific progress. This was political propaganda used to turn public opinion against the Church and was not based on fact.

Later, humanist supporters of Darwinian evolution led further accusations against the Church for being against scientific progress. Christians who challenged humanists trying to use Darwin's theories to prove that God did not exist were labelled critics of science itself. As is seen in humanist publications, this is a common attitude even nowadays.

EXAGGERATED INFLUENCE OF HUMANISM IN SCIENCE

Modern humanists suggest that becoming a scientist would require someone to renounce their faith as they believe it is impossible to be a scientist and hold a belief in God. However, the extent of humanist influence in science is somewhat exaggerated. Many scientists today are Christians and are motivated by their faith to discover more of God and His creation through their scientific research. One such person is the American geneticist, Dr. Francis Collins, one of the world's leading scientists and head of the Human Genome Project. He states: "I think God gave us an opportunity through the use of science to understand the natural world."

Further evidence of Christians embracing science is seen in a 2014 study by Rice University and the American Association for the Advancement of Science. It was discovered that 61% of the twelve million scientists in America considered themselves Christian. Only 24.4% could classify themselves as humanist, atheist or agnostic. Another interesting finding was that those scientists who would describe themselves as evangelical Christian (about two million scientists), were more serious and active in their faith than evangelical Christians who were not scientists. A possible explanation for this is that their scientific work has strengthened their faith and commitment to God, rather than challenged it.

"The first gulp from the glass of natural sciences will make you an atheist, but at the bottom of the glass God is waiting for you."

attributed to Werner Heisenberg, German physicist (1901-1976)

WHAT CHRISTIANS BELIEVE ABOUT SCIENCE

Christians believe that God created the universe and that science is the systematic study of the physical and natural realm through observations and experiments. Science is about acquiring knowledge and understanding of *how* things work, not about *why* they exist. It is the discovery of natural "laws", that reflect the orderly way in which God chooses to govern the natural universe (for example, the law of gravity) and which allow the prediction of events based on these laws. God, in His sovereign power, can overrule these "laws" whenever He chooses, and then we see miracles occurring.

While science deals with physical and natural things that can be measured, Christianity deals with the spiritual and supernatural - things which cannot be easily measured. Christianity is about the understanding of, belief in and relationship with a triune God. Science and Christianity are not mutually exclusive, as both are necessary to our understanding of the world. Science tries to answer the "how" questions. Christianity tries, through a personal relationship with God, to answer the spiritual questions that science does not address - questions such as: Why we do we exist? What is the meaning of life? What is our purpose on earth? What happens when I die? How can I be saved? There are many things that the Bible cannot answer about the physical world, while there is much in the spiritual realm that science cannot tackle. Science and Christianity are not opposed to each other. Rather, both should work together to gain a better understanding of God, the universe He made, and our place within it.

Many Church groups and denominations work towards a good relationship with the scientific community.

The Book of Discipline (2012) of the United Methodist Church, which outlines Methodist doctrine and beliefs, states:
Science and theology are complementary rather than mutually incompatible. We therefore encourage dialogue between the scientific and theological communities and seek the kind of participation that will enable humanity to sustain life on earth and, by God's grace, increase the quality of our common lives together.

The Episcopal Church's Catechism of Creation states:
Science and Christian theology can complement one another in the quest for truth and understanding. Together they can create a more complete understanding of and give greater meaning to our world.

The Catholic Catechism, which outlines the doctrine and beliefs of the Roman Catholic Church, states:
Methodical research in all branches of knowledge, provided it is carried out in a truly scientific manner and does not override moral laws, can never conflict with the faith, because the things of the world and the things the of the faith derive from the same God.

CHRISTIANS MUST EMBRACE SCIENCE

Like humanism, Christianity promotes rational thought and reason. Indeed, God introduces Himself in John's Gospel as the divine Word, the *logos* – reason itself. God invites Isaiah to reason together with Him (Isaiah 1:18). Christians also believe that things must be tested and proved. In 1 Thessalonians 5:21, the Bible tells us "test them all; hold on to what is good" So it is our responsibility and duty to seek the truth in all things, both natural and supernatural. Science is about logical thinking and using our God-given minds to discover things. In Jeremiah 33:2-3 we read:

> *This is what the Lord says, he who made the earth, the Lord who formed it and established it—the Lord is his name:*
>
> *'Call to me and I will answer you and tell you great and unsearchable things you do not know.'*

God, who is the creator of the world, invites us to call upon Him and He is pleased to answer us and reveal Himself and His wonders to us.

GENERAL AND SPECIAL REVELATION

God has revealed Himself in two main ways. The first is through nature and the universe, This is called general revelation. Psalm 19:1-4 says:

> *The heavens declare the glory of God;*
> *the skies proclaim the work of his hands.*
> *Day after day they pour forth speech;*
> *night after night they reveal knowledge.*
> *They have no speech, they use no words;*
> *no sound is heard from them.*
> *Yet their voice goes out into all the earth,*
> *their words to the ends of the world.*

This is supported by other verses such as Romans 1:20

> *For since the creation of the world God's invisible qualities—his eternal power and divine nature—have been clearly seen, being understood from what has been made, so that people are without excuse.*

and Acts 17:24-27

> *The God who made the world and everything in it is the Lord of heaven and earth and does not live in temples built by human hands. And he is not served by human hands, as if he needed anything. Rather, he himself gives everyone life and breath and everything else. From one man he made all the nations, that they should inhabit the whole earth; and he marked out their appointed times in history and the boundaries of their lands. God did this so that they would seek him and perhaps reach out for him and find him, though he is not far from any one of us.*

These verses tell us a number of things. First and foremost, they tell us that God exists, and secondly, that God created the universe, the earth and everything in them. The verses also tell us that God can be "clearly seen" and "understood" by observing nature and the universe. This is a clear invitation for Christians and the Church to support and encourage scientific exploration and discovery.

The second way in which God reveals Himself is called special revelation. This is the revelation of God through scripture and supremely through the incarnation, life, death, resurrection and ascension of the Lord Jesus Christ, as described in Hebrews 1:1-4.

CHECKING THE FACTS

As Christians we should not just accept what we are told or taught but should investigate things ourselves. There are many different theories and doctrines that both humanists and Christians teach. Some are based on facts and some are not. We should also be careful that we do not spread teachings that may be false. For example, Christians often share posts on social media such as Facebook without checking the facts. If we are moved to defend Christianity we must use accurate and credible information. We should also do so in a loving way, as love is core to our faith. How we say things is sometimes just as important as what we say.

"Will we turn our backs on science because it is perceived as a threat to God, abandoning all the promise of advancing our understanding of nature and applying that to the alleviation of suffering and the betterment of humankind? Alternatively, will we turn our backs on faith, concluding that science has rendered the spiritual life no longer necessary, and that traditional religious symbols can now be replaced by engravings of the double helix on our altars?

"Both of these choices are profoundly dangerous. Both deny truth. Both will diminish the nobility of humankind. Both will be devastating to our future. And both are unnecessary. The God of the Bible is also the God of the genome. He can be worshipped in the cathedral or in the laboratory. His creation is majestic, awesome, intricate and beautiful - and it cannot be at war with itself. Only we imperfect humans can start such battles. And only we can end them."

— Francis S. Collins, *The Language of God: A Scientist Presents Evidence for Belief (2006)*

7
HUMANISM, CHRISTIANITY AND CREATION

In the previous chapter we learnt that God reveals Himself to us in two ways: general revelation and special revelation. General revelation is God revealing Himself to us through nature and the universe. Special revelation is the revelation of God through scripture and through Jesus Christ. General revelation and special revelation should reinforce each other. In other words what we know about God from Scripture should be supported by what can be seen and observed in nature.

However, sometimes general and special revelation appear to contradict each other. Perhaps the best example of this are the two Biblical accounts of creation in Genesis 1 and 2 and how they compare to a number scientific theories regarding the age of the universe. A literal interpretation of the Bible and Genesis 1 and 2 would suggest the universe was created in six days or 144 hours between 6,000-10,000 years ago. However, scientific evidence suggests the universe is about 14 billion years old and the earth about 4.5 billion years old. One way to respond to this is to say that the Bible is right and that science is wrong. Another way is to say that the Bible is wrong and science is right. This approach may cause conflict between the scientific sector and the Church, or even within Christian communities. As we saw in the previous chapter, science and the Church can learn from each other. How the universe, our planet and the species which live on it came into being are very contentious issues. Christians should not shy away from discussing such matters, but should investigate the various theories and claims to help make up their own minds.

WHAT HUMANISTS BELIEVE

Humanists believe that the universe came into existence through natural means. As they do not believe in God they do not think that there was an external, divine influence in the creation of the universe, the world or humankind. Rather they believe that the universe came into existence through a natural event. They believe that life began through a series of random events and has evolved gradually through a process called natural selection over millions of years. Humans are seen as physical beings without a soul or spirit.

Much of humanist understanding of the universe is based on the theories and studies that began with the British naturalist and geologist Charles Darwin (1809-1882). Darwin, through a series of observations, most notably during a visit to the Galapagos Islands, proposed that all life was descended from the same ancestors. He suggested that species evolved by natural selection to suit their environments. Darwin put forward his ideas in a book called *On the Origin of Species* in 1859. He was not the first to have these ideas but he popularised them. Humanists have used his theories to support their own belief that life was not created by God. Darwin himself never explicitly rejected the existence of God though he may have been an agnostic.

WHY ARE MANY CHRISTIANS OPPOSED AND HOSTILE TO EVOLUTION?

Many Christians have been taught to believe that evolution is opposed to what the Bible says about creation, and that a believer cannot accept evolution and also believe in God. The terms "evolution" and "creation" are themselves problematic. Evolution does not necessarily exclude the existence of a creator God who initiated and guided the process. It is the humanist view of evolution which believes that the universe, earth and humankind came into existence without the intervention of God. This is a belief system that perhaps is better described as "evolutionism" or "naturalism".

The term creationism is often used to describe a belief in the literal interpretation of the creation process as described in Genesis 1 and 2. However, the term creationism is somewhat problematic because there are other Christians who believe in a form of evolution and also believe in God as creator.

In this chapter we will explore some of the differing points of view within the Christian community on this matter. What is important to note is that although there are so many different opinions, believing one theory over another does not affect your salvation as a Christian through the death and resurrection of the Lord Jesus Christ.

YOUNG EARTH THEORIES

There are some creation theories which teach that the earth is young. Young Earth creationists believe that the accounts of creation in Genesis 1 and 2 happened exactly as described. This view takes what is known as a literal interpretation of the Bible. Genesis 1 and 2 are seen as historical and scientific accounts of how the universe was created. They believe that the universe, the earth and humankind were created in six days and that God rested on the seventh day. By looking at the various genealogies and ages of people who lived in the Bible, Young Earth theorists calculate the Earth to be between 6, 000 and 10,000 years old.

Scientists do not support a Young Earth position because there are many things such as fossil remains and geological formations that seem to point to the universe and the earth being far older. Young Earth theories explain geological formations, fossil accounts and dinosaurs in many different ways. One explanation is that God created an earth and universe that looked as if they were already very old. They argue that, just as God created Adam fully grown, so He created the universe and the earth fully formed, as if earth had a long history. Another Young Earth explanation is that the flood described in Genesis chapters 6-9 caused the geological formations (mountains, valleys, canyons) that are seen on earth today. The flood also accounts for the fossil record as many species, such as dinosaurs, were wiped out during the flood and their remains preserved in the mud and sediment left afterwards. Young Earth theory says that "micro-evolution" is possible, for example some variations within species such as different breeds of dogs, but they reject the idea of "macro-evolution" creating whole new species by natural selection.

GAP THEORIES

A variation on the Young Earth theory are the Gap theories. One theory suggests that Genesis 1 and 2 happened at separate times. God created the universe in six days as in Genesis 1 and then rested on the seventh day. A long period passed during this rest. It was at this time that dinosaurs lived and died. Much later, God did a second creation process which is described in Genesis 2. In this second phase of creation, He created Adam and Eve and gave them and humankind spirits and souls.

Another theory suggests the six days of creation may have been scattered over a period of millions or billions of years, with vast gaps of time between them, thus making the earth as old as it appears to be.

A further theory says there was a gap in creation between Genesis 1:1 and the rest of the creation story as is told in Genesis 1 verse 2 onwards. According to this theory, God created the whole universe, but without humankind at first. It was during this time that Satan and his followers rebelled against God. They were cast from heaven and down to earth causing much death and destruction and resulting in the dinosaurs being killed. The earth was plunged into chaos (Genesis 1:2). God then restored the earth through the events as described in the rest of Genesis 1 and 2. The various Gap theories have some scientific flaws and have fallen out of favour with many Christians over the years.

INTELLIGENT DESIGN

Intelligent Design theory has become popular since the 1980s. Theorists believe that it is possible to detect God's active intervention in nature. The theory states that there are things in nature and in living organisms that are too complex to have developed through the process of natural selection, even over millions of years. Theorists believe that these complexities can only be a result of "intelligent design". In other words, life, or the universe, could not have come into existence by chance but was created by some form of intelligent being. Intelligent Design theorists point to such things as the human eye and DNA structure as examples of things too complex to have developed randomly. Intelligent Design theorists make use of science to try to prove their hypothesis. They oppose the humanist concept of "naturalism" which claims that nature is all that exists and that there is no God who acts in or through nature.

Intelligent Design is a popular and well supported theory amongst many Christians. However, humanists call Intelligent Design pseudoscience, or false science, as they do not feel that Intelligent Design theorists provide enough evidence to support their claims. There are many arguments made by Intelligent Design theorists which science cannot yet explain. However, some scientists dispute the theory as a whole. Scientists would argue that many "designs" are flawed, such as the useless human appendix that can cause death if it becomes inflamed.

OLD EARTH THEORY

Old Earth theory is gaining support amongst many Christians. Old Earth theorists believe that God is a creator God and that He reveals Himself through the natural world. They reject the idea that the universe is self-existing and self-sustaining. They believe that God holds the universe and natural world together through a set of universal or natural laws such as gravity. They also believe that God is supernatural and exists outside of the rules and laws of nature. They say that God is active in His creation and throughout human history and performs acts and miracles that cannot be explained through natural means. They believe that science is key to understanding and describing God's creation. However, it is not the only means to explain our existence. Christianity and science can work together to understand God more. The Old Earth theory suggests that God created the universe, the earth and life through a process that took billions of years. The theorists therefore believe in a God-ordained and God-guided process of evolution. They believe that humans are spiritual and physical creatures. They believe that Scripture is inspired by God and is infallible, but that some passages should be interpreted figuratively, symbolically or contextually and not literally. So the first chapters of Genesis are still theologically relevant and accurate but their purpose was to describe God as a creator and His love and provision for humankind rather than a historical and scientific account of creation.

WHAT SHOULD WE BELIEVE?

There are many more theories by Christians and non-Christians alike about how the universe came into existence. It is perhaps one of the oldest questions we have as the human race. Christians have been debating it for centuries. Even early Church theologians like Basil of Caesarea (330-379 AD) and Augustine of Hippo (354-430 AD) said that the six days described in Genesis may not be six literal days.

Augustine in the fifth century wrote on Genesis:

In matters that are so obscure and far beyond our vision, we find in Holy Scripture passages which can be interpreted in very different ways without prejudice to the faith we have received. In such cases, we should not rush in headlong and so firmly take our stand on one side that, if further progress in the search for truth justly undermines this position, we too fall with it.

Old Earth theorists, scientists and humanists use many similar terms when describing how evolution happens. None of these terms disproves the existence of God but they are used to describe what happens in nature over time.

Natural selection

Natural selection is the process described by Charles Darwin as the main method of evolutionary change. Some individuals in a population (a local group of animals or plants) will have more surviving offspring than other individuals do. That could be because they grow bigger, run faster to catch prey, are better camouflaged against predators, have flowers more attractive to bees for pollination, or many other reasons. Some of these differences could be due to the environment, for example, more food when young could make an animal grow bigger. But size or any other difference could also be due to genes, which are inherited. So the genes of the parents who produce more surviving offspring will be slightly more frequent in the next generation. The genetic make-up of the population as a whole has slightly changed and so has their average size or speed or the look of their camouflage or flowers. When this is repeated over many generations, large changes can be created.

Artificial selection

Darwin used the term "natural selection" to contrast with "artificial selection". Artificial selection is the age-old process of selective breeding in which humans deliberately try to create new variations or improvements in dogs or cattle or race-horses or crops or flowers, for example. The breeders select the parents carefully, hoping that the offspring will inherit the characteristics they want.

Survival of the fittest

This means "survival of those who are best at surviving". They might survive because they are strong or can run fast. Or they might survive because they have harder shells, are small enough to hide under stones so they don't get eaten, or many other reasons that are nothing to do with being "fit" in the sense of healthy. In natural selection, it is the survivors who live long enough to reproduce that contribute their genes to the next generation.

THE BIBLE REVEALS GOD'S CHARACTER AND RELATIONSHIP WITH HUMANKIND

There are many parts in the Bible that can be confusing and which people have interpreted differently. The Bible tells us that God created the world out of nothing by His own power and choice. But that does not necessarily mean that Genesis is a science text book. For example the creation accounts in Genesis 1 and 2 seem to give a different order of events. In Genesis 1 Adam was created after the plants while in Genesis 2 he is created before the plants. In various places writers of the Bible used metaphors and symbolism to make certain points. One example of this is in Isaiah 55:12 where the mountains will sing and the trees shall clap their hands. The Bible also does not always tell history in chronological order but some events are rearranged to make theological points. What is important is that we search the Bible to reveal who God is. The Bible is a book that reveals the character of God, humans' need of salvation, and how God has worked in time, space and history. It is about God's relationship with humankind and perhaps answers the deeper question, not of how we came to exist but why we were created.

There are two widely used statements of faith within the Christian community: the Apostles' Creed and the Nicene Creed (see chapter 15). These date back to the early Church. Both help us understand the core beliefs of the Christian faith and both begin with God being a creator God.

The Apostles' Creed begins:
I believe in God, the Father Almighty, Creator of Heaven and earth

The Nicene Creed begins:
I believe in one God, the Father Almighty, Maker of heaven and earth, and of all things visible and invisible. And in one Lord Jesus Christ, the only-begotten Son of God, begotten of the Father before all worlds; God of God, Light of Light, very God of very God; begotten, not made, being of one substance with the Father, by whom all things were made.

8

WHAT HUMANISTS BELIEVE ABOUT GOD, JESUS AND THE BIBLE

As Christians we must know what the differences are between our beliefs and the beliefs of humanists. We must also know which things are core to our faith.

GOD AND THE TRINITY

What Christians Believe

Christians believe in the Trinity, the God who is three persons in one. He is God the Father, Son and Holy Spirit. All three persons of the Trinity are equal and all are completely God. This is difficult to understand with our minds but we accept it through faith. Although the Bible never uses the word "Trinity", this teaching is clear in verses such as Matthew 28:19 and 2 Corinthians 13:14.

What Humanists Believe

Humanists believe that there is not enough evidence for them to accept the existence of God or the supernatural. And so they do not believe in God, or any form of the Trinity.

JESUS CHRIST

What Christians Believe

As Christians we follow Jesus Christ and worship Him as God. He is the second person of the Trinity. We believe that He always existed with the Father and the Spirit. He came to earth, was born to the Virgin Mary and lived a sinless life as a human. He died on the cross for the forgiveness of our sins. Afterwards He rose from the dead and ascended into heaven. He will return to judge all of humankind.

What Humanists Believe

Humanists do not believe that Jesus is God. Some believe that he is a myth and did not actually exist, even as a man. Others accept that there is evidence that there was a man called Jesus who lived about 2000 years ago. Some humanists state that there are elements of Jesus' teachings which inspire people to live better lives. Some even go as far as to call him a humanist. However, they reject any claims of Jesus' divinity, miracles or resurrection.

THE HOLY SPIRIT

What Christians Believe

The Holy Spirit is the third person of the Trinity and so He is God. The Holy Spirit was sent to continue what Christ did while He was on earth. The Spirit's purpose is to guide us and point us to Jesus and confirms through history that Jesus Christ is Lord. The Spirit is the one who evokes and maintains living faith (John 16:7-15). He can also give spiritual gifts as in 1 Corinthians 12 and make us more like Jesus in the way we live and think as in Galatians 5:22-24.

What Humanists Believe

The humanists say very little about the Holy Spirit except that God does not exist and that there is no supernatural realm.

THE BIBLE IS THE WORD OF GOD

What Christians Believe

The Bible is God's Word to humans. God used many different writers to write both the Old Testament and the New Testament, but all of them were inspired by the Holy Spirit as they wrote. The Bible is infallible, meaning that every part of it is completely true and without error. Nothing should be added or taken away from it. (See chapter 14.)

What Humanists Believe

Humanists reject the claim that the Bible is the word of God. They are convinced the book was written by humans without the influence of any divine inspiration. They believe that the Bible was written by superstitious people for superstitious people who lived in a cruel age. They believe that it contains many errors and contradictions. Some humanists say that although there are some good moral teachings in the Bible there are many more harmful teachings which promote violence or cause people to believe in something that does not exist. Humanists hold similar positions about other religious texts such as the Quran.

SALVATION

What Christians Believe

Salvation means being saved from eternal punishment for our sins. We are reconciled with God and when we die we will go to heaven to spend eternity in His presence. God loves us and gives salvation as a free gift, though none of us deserves it. This is known as being saved by grace. It is only possible because Jesus, the second person of the

Trinity, died for our sins so that we can be forgiven. Salvation cannot be earned and we do not have to work for it, though in gratitude and love for Him we must live according to God's Word. If we believe in Jesus Christ our sins are forgiven and we receive eternal life.

What Humanists Believe

Humanists do not believe that there are eternal consequences for our actions. They say that there is no God, judgement, heaven, hell or any kind of afterlife. There is therefore nothing to be saved from except humankind's extinction. Humanists think that people who believe in salvation are deluded and victims of their religious upbringing. Humanists say that having a belief in a saviour or a hope of salvation is dangerous as it takes people's attention off the problems of the present. Humanists state that humankind is responsible for its own survival as a species and its own form of secular salvation.

HUMAN BEINGS

What Christians Believe

Christians believe that humans are created by God in His image. We are all equal in the eyes of God and are His children. We can have a personal and living relationship with God. We have been created for a purpose which is to glorify God and to bring others to know the freedom of a relationship with God. We are also to influence the world through love and seeking justice for the poor, vulnerable and oppressed. Humans are physical and spiritual beings. Death is the separation of the physical and spiritual. If someone accepts Jesus Christ as Lord and Saviour they will spend eternity with Him.

What Humanists Believe

Humanists believe that humankind is a result of an unguided evolutionary process. They hold that humankind is the pinnacle of existence, and that no form of life is higher than humankind. Humanists say that humans are merely natural and have only physical bodies. So when someone dies they simply cease to exist. They do not feel that there is any purpose to our existence besides survival.

Secular humanism is a branch within humanism with an even stronger focus on removing all religion and God from society. This is how it is defined by the Council for Secular Humanism:

"We can now attempt our definition of secular humanism. Secular humanism begins with atheism (absence of belief in a deity) and agnosticism or skepticism (epistemological caution that rejects the transcendent as such due to a lack of evidence). Because no transcendent power will save us, secular humanists maintain that humans must take responsibility for themselves. While atheism is a necessary condition for secular humanism, it is not a sufficient one. Far from living in a moral vacuum, secular humanists "wish to encourage wherever possible the growth of moral awareness and the capacity for free choice and an understanding of the consequences thereof."

SIN

What Christians Believe

Christians believe that all humans are born with a sinful nature due to what theologians call "original sin". None of us can lead sinless lives. We believe God is holy and because of our sinful nature we fall short of His holy standards. We could be eternally separated from God because of sin. However, the Father sent His Son Jesus Christ to die in payment for our sin. By this act of love we are forgiven from our sin and are cleansed. Through the sacrifice of Jesus and the help of the Holy Spirit we are freed from our sinful nature and can become more Christ-like and sinless in our thoughts, actions and words.

As Christians we also believe in Satan and his spiritual followers who strive to bring evil, chaos and destruction into the world. Although humans are responsible for their own actions Satan is able to influence people to commit evil.

What Humanists Believe

Humanists reject the idea of a sinful nature and believe that humans are naturally good. Humanists think that Christians must be guilt-ridden because they will always feel sinful. They also believe that there are no absolute right or wrongs. What might be considered wrong or sinful by one person may not be wrong for another person. It is up to each person to decide what is right and wrong for themselves. Humanists do not believe in the spiritual realm and so they do not think that anyone can be influenced by the Holy Spirit to do good or by Satan to do evil.

SEXUALITY AND MARRIAGE

What Christians Believe

Christians believe that God created sex. God has two purposes for sex. The first is to have children. In Genesis 1:28 God tells Adam and Eve: "Be fruitful and increase in number." The second purpose is for emotional and physical intimacy. A sexual relationship is to be kept within the boundaries of marriage. Marriage is a symbolic representation of the faithful relationship God has with the Church. Sex and marriage build a oneness where two people come together to form one.

Most Christians also believe that man and woman are created and designed to need each other's complementary traits. Therefore homosexual and lesbian practices are not approved by the Bible. But Christians must respect and love all people, regardless of their sexual orientation, because all people are respected and loved by God.

What Humanists Believe

Humanists have a very liberal view of sexuality and marriage. They believe that religions such as Christianity have restricted and repressed sexual conduct. They believe one of the mandates of humanism is to free humankind from these restrictions. And so any sexual expression and exploration between consenting adults is encouraged, including premarital sex, homosexuality and lesbianism, pornography and adultery. Sex education for children, teaching them sexual freedom and activity, is applauded. The absolute right to abortion in all circumstances is also promoted. Humanists believe that the traditional family unit does not work for everyone and that people should be encouraged to build a family structure that suits them.

Rules for American Schools about Transgender Students
In May 2016 the U.S. Departments of Education and Justice wrote a letter to explain the obligations of American schools (including colleges and universities) under Title IX of the Education Amendments of 1972. (See pages 180-187 for full text of the letter.) Title IX prohibits sex discrimination, and the letter explained what schools must do to make sure that transgender students are not discriminated against. It said that schools should treat transgender students according to their gender identity and allow them access to sex-segregated activities and facilities (for example, restrooms, locker rooms, showers, housing, athletic teams) even if it made other people uncomfortable. The school must follow whatever sense of internal gender the individual student said they had, without asking for any documentation or proof of medical diagnosis or treatment. Schools who do not comply could have their federal funding stopped, but educational institutions controlled by religious organisations are exempt if these rules would conflict with their religious beliefs.

Asking British Parents to Help their Pre-School Children to Choose their Gender

In April 2016 Brighton and Hove City Council wrote to many families with four-year-old children to tell them which school their child had been enrolled in. They asked the parents or carers to fill in a pupil registration form, which had a tick-box to specify whether the child was male or female. But a note alongside the tick-box said, "We recognise that not all children and young people identify with the gender they were assigned at birth or may identify as a gender other than male or female, however the current systems (set nationally) only record gender as male or female. Please support your child to choose the gender they most identify with. Or, if they have another gender identity please leave this blank and discuss with your child's school."

9
THE CHURCH AND THE WORLD

The humanist debate and the Church's responses to it are ultimately about the role of the Church in the world, the influence of culture on the Church, and the influence of the Church on culture. The question of whether Christians should get involved in worldly affairs has raged for centuries. It has divided the Church; it has generated denominations, great mission and evangelistic movements; it has toppled empires and changed the course of the world. Yet, despite this history, or possibly because of it, the Church still struggles to understand its role within the world.

The Church is not a building, or an organisation, or even leaders within a denomination. It is made up of individual believers who belong to a community, a fellowship, a communion of saints. When we speak of the Church, its role in the world, its challenges, failings, responsibilities and mission we must understand that this refers directly to us. We cannot wait and hope for other Christians or our church leaders to rise up to the challenge. It is up to each one of us individually as well as a community of believers to bring the change the world so desperately needs.

HAVING A FORM OF GODLINESS BUT DENYING ITS POWER

As we have learnt throughout this book, the Christian morality that was so widespread in some societies just a short while ago has been attacked and eroded by a humanist agenda. Many consider modern society and even the Church to be in a state of moral crisis.

Society is shaped by humanist concepts such as existentialism, a philosophy which emphasises individual existence, freedom and choice. It expresses the view that human beings live in an irrational universe, that life has no essential purpose and that we must make our own meaning by exercising personal freedom and choice. People with this worldview believe that they are not answerable to anyone but themselves. In such societies people pursue experiences, pleasure and instant gratification. It is all about the here and now, and about looking and feeling good. Other terms can also be used to describe aspects of a humanist society: narcissism (to love oneself above all else); hedonism (the pursuit of sensual pleasure and avoidance of any discomfort); relativism (having no absolute truth); and postmodernism (living according to what you feel is right for you). In societies which are influenced by these ways of thinking, where right and wrong are considered merely relative, some injustices and sins are ignored or overlooked, and some are even celebrated. The Church has not been immune from this and there are elements within the Church that have been influenced by this prevailing humanist culture.

> "[The head offices in London of the worldwide Anglican Church are being used] as instruments to cajole orthodox Global South provinces of the Communion into acquiescence with the secular sexual culture which has made such inroads into the Anglican Churches of the West."
>
> **Most Rev. Dr Eliud Wabukala, Archbishop of Kenya (2016) referring to the issue of same-sex marriage**

The state of society and of some parts of the Church seems to smack of the warning in 2 Timothy 3:1-5:

> *But mark this: there will be terrible times in the last days. People will be lovers of themselves, lovers of money, boastful, proud, abusive, disobedient to their parents, ungrateful, unholy, without love, unforgiving, slanderous, without self-control, brutal, not lovers of the good, treacherous, rash, conceited, lovers of pleasure rather than lovers of God — having a form of godliness but denying its power. Have nothing to do with such people.*

As a Christian community and as individual Christians we must be continually alert for negative elements of humanism and modern culture that may have crept into our thinking and way of living. One example is the way in which humanism teaches us always to think well of ourselves and to suppress any feeling of guilt. Yet, when we have done wrong, guilt is the right reaction and this painful feeling leads us to repentance and restoration of our relationship with God and if necessary with our fellow human beings. Another example is shame, which used to be an important guiding factor in behaviour, dress and lifestyle. But modern Western society admires boldness and shamelessness, condemning modest people as prudes. In their desire to be relevant to contemporary society and culture, many Christians are embracing the humanist attitude of shamelessness.

THE CHURCH AND CULTURE

Throughout history, churches and Christians have typically approached living in a culture in three main ways:

The Separation Approach
A church can choose to remove itself from the world and focus completely and exclusively on spiritual matters and the church's ministry to its members. This approach ensures that they are not influenced or tainted by the prevailing culture, because they are not exposed to it. In such a church, Christians avoid as much contact with the world as

possible. Others, while continuing to live in the world, view spiritual life and worldly life as completely separate.

Dangers of Separation

The danger of this approach is that the Church hands over its civil responsibility and moral authority to society and the State. When Christian communities do not act on Christ's commands to be "salt" and "light" in the world but instead hand over their moral authority and responsibility to others (such as governments or secular charities), then they allow institutions and powerful individuals in society the potential to make unjust decisions and to act in ungodly ways. Then both the Church and society are in danger of moral decay, which ultimately may be a factor leading to the collapse of society.

Another danger occurs when the Church has separated itself from the world to such an extent that it either directly or indirectly supports evil by its separation. The German church in the 1930s is an example of this. The Church believed that the inner spiritual world and the outer natural world could be kept apart, so the Church and its members should only focus on spiritual things and not be concerned with political or worldly things. Christians could be members of the Church and also members of the Nazi party because they were two separate worlds. This is how devotion to Hitler, the Nazi party, the Aryan race and the German "fatherland" could exist in the Church without most individuals feeling any internal moral conflict.

The Barmen Declaration 1934

Almost at the same time as the 1933 *Humanist Manifesto* was being drafted, a group of courageous German Christians, led by Karl Barth and Dietrich Bonhoeffer, were formulating what became known as the Barmen Declaration, with its affirmation that Jesus Christ is Lord. The Declaration was released in 1934. It rebuked the wider German Church for being submissive to the German state and ignoring, or even endorsing, the Nazi ideology which was so obviously contrary to the Gospel. The Declaration went on to affirm the authority of Jesus Christ, His Word and Spirit over all things in the world including powers, principalities and culture. It stated that the Church must examine itself and repent of allowing itself to focus on church matters and appear godly while failing to challenge ideologies in the world that were obviously ungodly. The Declaration called for a renewal of the Church. It was an appeal to the Church to seek its true identity, reclaim its morality and stand against the injustices of the day. Those who drafted the Declaration called upon the Church to be a "Confessing Church", meaning one which proclaimed truth and rejected false doctrines.

Sadly the German Church at large took no notice of the Declaration. The evil of Hitler and the Nazi Party was permitted to flourish unchecked resulting in a world war and a holocaust in which tens of millions of people perished. The Declaration, however, did much to reform the Church across Europe after the War.

"The Church is the State" Approach

The second attitude the Church can take is at the opposite extreme to the first. With this approach there is no separation between Church and State. Instead the Church becomes overly involved in the governance of society. The Church is the State. The advantage of this is that the Church is active in all aspects of culture and society.

Dangers of the State and Church Being One

However, as history has taught us, this approach has many pitfalls. Fundamentally, it fails to distinguish between the "things of Caesar" and the "things of God", as Jesus taught us to do (Luke 20:25); instead the Church claims all things for itself.

In order to govern a country or community the Church needs to wield absolute power and enforce its will on citizens. When this happens the Church tends to become corrupted by political ambition, a quest for absolute power, pride and greed. Torture, inquisitions and burnings at the stake have often followed when the Church is so closely aligned with the State.

Politicians and dictators often seek the support of a Church, or create a State Church, in order to legitimise their leadership. A good example of this is apartheid South Africa, where the Dutch Reformed Church was so strongly affiliated with the State that it began to use theology and spiritual justification to support and endorse the oppressive actions of the State. In such situations it becomes very difficult to challenge injustices and atrocities because it means not only challenging the State but, by implication, God Himself. A more recent example is modern day Zimbabwe where some elements of the Church are endorsing and supporting the dictator-led government in exchange for political and financial favour.

It is, of course, right that the Church be involved in the political and public space but only as a guide and to provide moral authority. The Church should have a significant role in developing and maintaining the moral framework in which society functions. Individual Christians should be encouraged to pursue political careers and Christian politicians should rule with integrity and a passion for justice. However, the Church as an institution and the State should remain separate.

The Contextualisation Approach

The third approach is where the Church intentionally or unintentionally becomes overly influenced by the prevailing culture. This is sometimes called contextualisation. There are some aspects of cultures that are useful and healthy and which should be celebrated or promoted. There are also some aspects of cultures that are not beneficial or right, and which should be questioned, challenged, changed or removed. And in between these two extremes there are some aspects which are neither harmful nor overtly positive and so a neutral stance may be taken about them.

The Church always exists in the context of a culture, but scripture must judge that culture and enable Christians to discern what is good, bad or neutral within it. Christians can use good or neutral aspects of culture to make the Gospel relevant to a society or a particular people group. Paul's speech on Mars Hill to the Athenians (Acts 17) is an example of helpful contextualisation. Paul's knowledge and awareness of the Athenian culture and religious beliefs gave his words credibility and "earned" him the right to be heard. However, Paul, in other writings is quick to rebuke the Church for allowing the values of the world's culture to have undue influence on Christian believers. His letter to the Galatians, where he questions the Church's unnecessary adherence to Jewish culture and tradition, is an example.

Christians must take note of developments and trends in the prevailing cultures or consciousness within societies. They must evolve and adapt their communication to ensure that the message of Christ remains relevant, but not at the expense of absolute truths or the fundamentals of our faith.

Dangers of Contextualisation

The experience of the Israelites in the Old Testament can be read as a warning about the dangers of conforming too much to the culture around us. This might be called over-contextualisation. As the Israelites became more and more influenced by the cultures of pagan nations their concept and understanding of God was affected – almost always in a damaging way.

Surely one of the most heartbreaking examples is that of Jephthah who sacrificed his own daughter so as not to break a vow he had made to God (Judges 11). Despite serving God and having been greatly used by God he was so influenced by the pagan culture in which he lived that his understanding of God was distorted. He made a vow that was against God's nature and laws. His daughter was sacrificed as a result of his misunderstanding of God's character. The moral compass Jephthah used to guide his actions was that of the pagan culture around him and not that of God's Word.

A verse that is repeated a number of times throughout the book of Judges is "In those days Israel had no king; all the people did whatever seemed right in their own eyes." Without absolute rights and wrongs and without being guided by our king, the Lord Jesus Christ, or by the Holy Spirit or by scripture, many societies today have drifted on to very dangerous ground.

Contextualisation Within the Church

As we have learnt throughout this book, humanism's rejection of God and its lack of moral absolutes have affected not only much of modern society but also many parts of the Church. There is a constant danger of falling too much under the sway of our surrounding culture without us even noticing it. Culture may subtly influence our understanding of the nature of God, as was the case with Jephthah, or we may make conscious decisions to embrace culture and its "norms" to such an extent that the absolutes of God and the truth of the Gospel become watered down.

We must maintain a strong link to scripture and Christian practices, ways of life and tradition (for example meeting regularly to break bread together in communion) while at the same time being aware of and relevant to the world in which we live.

Contextualisation Must Not Compromise the Gospel and Truth

In today's increasingly humanist, liberal and politically correct society there exists a growing assumption within some Churches that all aspects of all cultures are good. This leads to a tendency to romanticise culture or to a feeling that no aspect of a culture can be criticised for fear of offending. Therefore some churches across the world have begun to accept things such as cohabitation before marriage, immodest dressing, same-sex marriage, taking or giving bribes, or even ancestor worship. Some churches are unresponsive to issues of injustice. Or in some instances the Church has become involved in campaigning for social justice but does not in a way that includes proclaiming the redeeming message of the Gospel, for fear of offending secularists or people of other religions. Rightly, issues such as sickness, hunger and poverty are tackled, but without the eternal spiritual healing and saving power of the Gospel those helped will forever remain lost, and the world will continue as a godless place.

But there is another way for the Church to approach the world and culture. This will be discussed in the next chapter.

10
THE CHRISTIAN IDENTITY

Christians living in the modern age are faced with the question of who they are. They no longer live in the age of Christendom, which gave identity to Christians. The age of Christian nations, which later defined them, is also gone. Western Christians now exist within pseudo-Christian societies, burdened with all the negative elements of past and present. Some embrace this, finding security in the history and tradition of Christianity in the West. Others reject it and are left with feelings of alienation and non-belonging. If the modern Christian is to have an identity, what should it be?

The New Testament speaks of the Christian community as a communion of saints, a fellowship of believers, strangers and pilgrims within this world, a new commonwealth. Given that Christians live in a physical world and are shaped by contemporary cultures, the nature of Christian identity could be founded on the following principles.

Christians are different from those around them. They are aliens passing through. Although they are in the world they are not of the world. They have a heavenly destination and have begun that heavenly life here on earth.

Christians make up a community of brothers and sisters, a community which transcends race, culture, clan, tribe and gender. This community, based on love, expresses itself visibly through truth, virtue and justice. This sets Christians apart from everyone else and gives them a primary duty towards their own, in addition to their responsibility towards the wider world.

This community of believers must have a way of life that is ruled by the Word of God and His divine law. This is not negative but immensely positive, for it is a pathway that leads to life. To divert from this pathway brings disaster and judgement.

CREATE AND CULTIVATE A NEW CULTURE

The previous chapter explored the three traditional approaches the Church has taken with regard to its place in the world and how it deals with the prevailing culture. Each approach has major disadvantages and pitfalls. There is a fourth way to approach living in the world and the issue of culture. That is for Christians to create and cultivate a culture. The Church must not ignore culture, separate itself from it, submit to it or copy it but must take a leading role in society so as to create a new, godly, better way of living and thinking. It must create and cultivate a new culture for itself, which will in turn have influence on the prevailing culture of society. This new culture must be marked by love but also by justice, righteousness and truth. The Church must take a leading, active role as part of the living world today. It can only do so by again becoming a "confessing church" that declares the truth, as Bonhoeffer and Barth proposed in 1934.

Declaring the Creed

The first step is for the Church to recognise the distinctive beliefs that set Christians apart from non-Christians. It must affirm its creed, that is, a brief formula of faith that all believers can affirm openly and declare to all people. Our creed separates us from the world. It is an identity marker for us.

In the Jewish religion the *shema* is an affirmation of Judaism and a declaration of faith in one God: "Hear, Israel, the Lord is our God. The

Lord is one." Following this pattern, the Islamic religion has the *shahada*, an affirmation of Islam and a declaration of faith in one God and that Muhammad is his messenger: "There is no god but Allah, and Muhammad is the messenger of Allah." In both religions there is a declaration as well as an affirmation on the unity of God and on the distinctiveness of the people of God. It is more than just a creed or statement of faith. It is an affirmation and a declaration of that faith to the world, marking out the believer and their beliefs as different.

Various Christian creeds have evolved in Christian history. In the New Testament there are passages that encapsulate the Christian faith. With the passage of time, other creeds were formulated to ward of specific heresies that had developed and to defend the truth. These explained the central theological doctrines of the Christian faith – truths that had to be accepted, believed and affirmed. But because of the complexity of the language needed to explain the theology, these creeds were not easy to declare in the same way as the *shema* and *shahada*. Furthermore, these creeds were not seen as setting the boundaries that would separate Christian people from the rest of the world. The Christian community today needs therefore to rediscover its Jewish roots and to have a creed which is both an affirmation and a declaration, which separates Christians from the world and sets out their identity as a chosen people with their own law, a holy (or separate) nation (1 Peter 2:9).

The Apostles' Creed and the Nicene Creed sum up the fundamentals of the Christian faith, as compiled by believers in the early period of the Church (see chapter 15). When the German Church faced the major challenge of Nazism, a section of the Church turned back to its historic creeds and also re-affirmed and declared the Lordship of Christ over culture in the words of the Barmen Declaration.

When the Church affirms that Jesus Christ is Lord, it is saying no to all the gods of the contemporary age. When the Church affirms the uniqueness of salvation, it is rejecting other philosophies that deny that fundamental truth. When the Church affirms the authority of scripture it rejects all other authorities, whether secular or spiritual, that impinge on the Church's faith.

But when sections of the Church embrace humanism, they deny the fundamentals of the creedal testimony that sums up their faith.

This creedal testimony is not just a thing of the past that we remember, but is a present reality that we affirm and live out. This may bring with it persecution and rejection. In the face of this, the Church will need courage, conviction and faith so as to stand firm.

Living in Community
The second step is for the Church to live out what it means to be a Church or community of believers. This is a concept that has deep and powerful meanings. Community was the first casualty of the Fall. In the Genesis story the first humans, Adam and Eve, broke their relationship with God and with each other. And so, re-establishing community with God and with each other can be seen as an important stage in reconciliation, healing and spiritual development, not just of individuals but of groups of peoples. A community reflects the model of the unity of the Trinity, the three-in-one.

Community allows us to join individually and with other believers in the divine communion between the Father, the Son and the Spirit. Community first and foremost is about belonging and identity. We find our common identity in Christ. Galatians 3:27-28 says: "For all of you who were baptised into Christ have clothed yourselves with Christ. There is neither Jew nor Gentile, neither slave nor free, nor is there male and female, for you are all one in Christ Jesus." Community defines who we are – God's children and members of one body. And as we find our identity in Christ there is an expectation of how we must live and act (Romans 12:1-2).

Community is About Commitment
Community is also about commitment to Christ and to righteousness. Mark 8:34-38 says:

> Then he called the crowd to him along with his disciples and
> said: "Whoever wants to be my disciple must deny themselves

There is one God in three persons

God *the all-powerful Creator and Sustainer*
our loving heavenly Father

God *the Son, Jesus Christ,*
incarnate Word,
our Redeemer and Lord

God *the Holy Spirit,*
Revealer of truth,
our divine Comforter

Hallelujah Hallelujah Hallelujah

*and take up their cross and follow me. For whoever wants to
save their life will lose it, but whoever loses their life for me
and for the gospel will save it. What good is it for someone
to gain the whole world, yet forfeit their soul? Or what can
anyone give in exchange for their soul? If anyone is ashamed
of me and my words in this adulterous and sinful generation,
the Son of Man will be ashamed of them when he comes in
his Father's glory with the holy angels.*

There is a direct challenge to each one of us to deny ourselves and
take up the cross of Christ. Other verses in the Bible say we must do
this daily. We must not be ashamed of Christ, His Gospel, His words
or commandments. Society's quest for status, ease, respectability and
comfort has created an unwillingness in the Church to embrace suffering
or disgrace for Christ. Yet these things were an essential of the teachings
of Jesus and often a daily experience in the lives of the early Christians.
Today suffering has become the unmentionable subject in self-absorbed,
contemporary Western Christianity, for it requires a denial of self and a
denial of the priorities of a society which seeks so diligently for outward
beauty, physical health, pleasure and affluence.

Community is also about commitment to our Christian brothers and
sisters. This involves an essential loyalty to them. We should never
betray our fellow Christians for any reason. Betrayal has become one
of the features of our humanist-dominated societies, where everyone
seeks their own welfare and good above that of others and above the
common good. People are willing to go to any lengths to achieve their
own goals and ambitions. The Christian community must show that it
is different, with values based on self-sacrifice, putting others first and
seeking their welfare.

Community is About Meeting Physical and Spiritual Needs

In practical terms, community is about creating a culture of love, respect,
responsibility, care, commitment, integrity, selfless living, and mutual
submission to each other. It is place where people grow, develop, are healed,
guided and gently corrected. It is a place of safety where people can be

honest and vulnerable without fear of rejection or shame. In community, needs are seen and met. In community the Church meets the needs of its poor, sick and vulnerable not just with spiritual balm but with physical help.

The early Christian community was known in society for its love of its own members, shown in practical care. Christians recognised that they were one community, one body, through which the blood of Jesus Christ flowed, and this placed on them a heavenly responsibility to care for one another. So if one part of the body hurt, the whole body hurt. This sense of belonging and identity meant that a Christian's family was the Christian community, who were nearer and dearer to them than their flesh and blood relatives.

The development of individualism in the West, coupled with the breakdown of both the extended family and the nuclear family, has meant that the Church now sees itself more as a collection of individuals, each with the sole concern to be personally blessed and helped, along with their nearest and dearest. Contented with their lives and on the way to heaven, each is self-seeking and self-satisfied.

Community is about Love, Truth, Righteousness and Justice

A community must always strive to find the balance between love and truth. In a community that is dominated by love and not truth, people are never corrected. They are allowed to continue in sin. Issues of injustice and righteousness are not addressed for fear of offending people or because people themselves do not want to change. People in this kind of community say that they live by grace and not by law. However, they forget that Jesus in Matthew 5 and 6 talks calls us to a higher standard of behaviour when we live in grace.

A community where truth dominates without much love is one that is harsh and dogmatic and can easily become a cult or sect.

In a community that lives in love and truth, people are lovingly corrected and guided, injustices are recognised and challenged, and there is a standard of righteousness to aspire to.

> "We tend culpably to evade our responsibility when we ought to instruct and admonish them [the ill-doers], sometimes even with sharp reproof and censure, either because the task is irksome, or because we are afraid of giving offence; or it may be that we shrank from incurring their enmity, for fear that they may hinder and harm us in worldly matters, in respect either of what we eagerly seek to attain, or of what we weakly dread to lose."
>
> Augustine of Hippo (c. 413)

If We Love One Another

It is through the model of a loving community that the world understands who we are as followers of Jesus. "By this everyone will know that you are my disciples, if you love one another" (John 13:35). Loving one another is also how the world should live. It is one of Jesus' commandments (John 15:12). If we are to change the world and create a culture for the world to adopt, then we, the Church, must first model it correctly, even though it may bring down persecution upon us. If we are not sure of our identity as Christians individually, and do not have a sense of belonging to a loving community of believers, how can we expect non-Christians to be attracted to join us?

Delighting in the Commandments of God

The final stage is obedience to all that God has commanded. Jesus says in John 14:15 that if we love Him we will obey Him. If we have a loving relationship with God we delight to keep His commandments. Jesus' commandments are not just about outward actions. They are more to do with making sure our hearts and minds are pure and renewed. This is very clear in Jesus' Sermon on the Mount in Matthew chapters 5, 6 and 7 which covers issues such as anger, lust, divorce, oaths, violence, reconciliation with enemies, giving, prayer and fasting.

Many of Jesus' commandments are about love: loving God (Matthew 22:37), our neighbour (Matthew 22:39), one another (John 13:34-35), and our enemies (Matthew 5:44).

Another commandment, which is sometimes called the Great Commission, is outlined in Matthew 28:18-20.

> Then Jesus came to them and said, "All authority in heaven and on earth has been given to me. Therefore go and make disciples of all nations, baptising them in the name of the Father and of the Son and of the Holy Spirit, and teaching them to obey everything I have commanded you. And surely I am with you always, to the very end of the age.

This call has many layers. It speaks of the need to tell others about the Gospel of Jesus and teach them how to follow Him. This means showing people how to live well under the authority of God. God has given us a set of guidelines in scripture for us all to live by. It is for our own good and for the good of the world. If we live by these guidelines we will find a sense of internal and external peace and wholeness called shalom. On a larger scale there are natural consequences for communities that choose to live in obedience. They will live in a context where people care for each other and where people feel safe and secure. It is in such environments that we as humans are able to thrive.

Some believe that the Great Commission is a call not only to reach out to individuals within the nations but also to the nations themselves. This could mean that the Church must look to influence whole countries, societies and governments.

Outward and Inward Obedience

As we have already seen, Jesus teaches us we must obey scripture not only through outward actions but also in our hearts and minds. Obedience starts with our attitude and willingness to be righteous. There are many places in the Bible where guidance or rules for right living are suggested. Paul in Galatians 4, 5 and 6 provides a useful study of how to live. He tells us that we have been set free from blind obedience to the laws, rules and norms of culture. We must be transformed within ourselves. If we let even a small part of the world influence us, it is like yeast in bread which could affect every part of us. Paul reminds us that Christ has set us free from the bondage of the law but we must not use this freedom to live in sin. In fact when we live by grace we are called to a higher standard.

Paul then lists some examples of sinful acts including sexual immorality, impurity, drunkenness, worshipping things rather than God, witchcraft, hatred, causing disunity, jealousy, fits of rage, selfish ambition. Other parts of the Bible list other types of sin such as lying, deceiving and spreading rumours to bring others down. Christians will readily agree with all this teaching, and yet in practice there is often a marked difference between what they believe and what they do. A new culture of hatred and destruction is permeating Christianity in many contexts, bringing with it a willingness to gossip, spread rumours, make false accusations, betray and work to destroy Christian believers and Christian ministries. In particular, there is a growing view that it is permissible for a Christian to lie if it will achieve objectives that they believe to be right. Often Christians use social media, and hide behind a cloak of anonymity, to do their work of attack and destruction. Those behaving like this may be prayerful, Bible-reading Christians who believe that they are doing the will of God.

> *I hate, I despise your religious festivals; your assemblies are a stench to me. Even though you bring me burnt offerings and grain offerings, I will not accept them. Though you bring choice fellowship offerings, I will have no regard for them. Away with the noise of your songs! I will not listen to the music of your harps. But let justice roll on like a river, righteousness like a never-failing stream!*
>
> **Amos 5:21-24**

Paul goes on in Galatians 5:22 to say that if we live by the Spirit our lives will show the fruit of the Spirit: love; joy; peace; patience; kindness; goodness; faithfulness; gentleness and self-control. He also mentions that we must do good to all people, especially other Christians.

Helping Others to Obey Commandments

Paul tells us that we must not only strive to live righteously ourselves but we also have a duty to help those around us to live like that too. We must gently, with love and without judgement, correct other Christians who are living in sin. Paul reminds us that by doing so we fulfil the law of Christ. This is discipleship. However, Paul warns that we cannot deceive or fool God by justifying our own sinful actions. Paul writes that God cannot be mocked. And so we cannot disciple others if we are not working to rid ourselves of the influences of the world. Thankfully we do not do this alone and we rely on the Word of God and the power of the Holy Spirit in our lives. If we seek God, are obedient and live by the Spirit, then the fruit of the Spirit, as mentioned above, will develop naturally and be seen in our lives.

> "The sacramental host of God's elect is warring still on earth, Jesus Christ being the Captain of their salvation. He has said, "Lo! I am with you alway, even unto the end of the world." Hark to the shouts of war! Now let the people of God stand fast in their ranks, and let no man's heart fail him. It is true that just now in England the battle is turned against us, and unless the Lord Jesus shall lift his sword, we know not what may become of the church of God in this land; but let us be of good courage, and play the man."
>
> **C.H. Spurgeon (1866)**

If the Church focuses on **Creed, Community and Commandments** then Christians will have their own strong identity. If they have their own strong Christian identity they will be able to transform the world's culture rather than finding themselves moulded by the world into its shape, even though they may face persecution for being different.

However, it must be remembered that we are the Church. The movement starts with us individually. We must seek the Lord's guidance and courage in our lives through prayer and scripture to take the necessary steps to transform ourselves first and then the world.

11
A CHALLENGE TO ALL BELIEVERS

THE MODEL OF THE EARLY CHURCH

The previous chapter explored the idea that the Church, instead of ignoring the world or succumbing to it, can take an active part in creating and nurturing a Christian culture within society. In order to do this the Church can use the steps of Creed, Community and Commandments to strengthen its own identity. Although we may feel it is impossible to make real, significant changes to the prevailing culture we must remember that all things are possible under the authority of Jesus Christ and through the help, power and guidance of the Holy Spirit.

The early Church and how it challenged the mighty yet morally corrupt Roman Empire is a wonderful example of the transforming power of the Gospel. The first Christians lived in a multicultural, multi-faith, pluralist context. There was Judaism, paganism and the worship of Pan, Baal, Greek and Roman gods. There was also the overarching power of the Roman Empire and the pagan Roman religion, including Emperor worship, which was largely based on humanism.

During the first three centuries AD the Church was very small and widely scattered throughout the Roman Empire which covered much of the known Western world and ruled with absolute power. The Church survived and kept its identity in this context by remaining different and by being willing to suffer because of its vulnerability and powerlessness. Christians at that time were not ashamed to be different, to identify with their crucified Lord and to carry the marks of the cross. For the early Church, Jesus Christ was the supreme Lord of history and of culture and there could be no compromise.

The greatest challenge that early Christianity faced came from the Roman religion in which the Roman emperor (Caesar) was worshipped as god. His divinity had to be acknowledged by all citizens and they were required to worship him publicly. The power of the Roman religion extended into all areas of life. The empire used the military to enforce this religion. Rome did permit the acknowledgement and worship of other gods and other religions so long as they admitted that Caesar was lord and god over all and as long as the other religions did not threaten his powerbase or worship of him.

The first British Christian martyr

According to tradition, Alban was a third century Romano-British citizen, who sheltered a Christian priest fleeing from persecution. Alban was moved by the priest's faith and courage and asked him for more information about Christianity, which was at that time a forbidden religion in the Roman Empire.

When the authorities came to arrest the priest, Alban exchanged clothes with him so that the priest escaped and Alban was arrested in his place and brought before the city magistrate. Alban refused to sacrifice to the emperor and the Roman gods, declaring: "I worship and adore the true and living God, who created all things." He was beheaded.

The Christian Church was faced with many questions and dilemmas about how they should practise Christianity in this context. If Caesar the man was god, then should Jesus Christ be seen as simply another deity under the Roman state? Or was Jesus supreme over the State? What of the laws and ceremonies of the State? Should they be accepted or rejected? What happened when those ceremonies and laws conflicted with the laws and teachings of the Christian faith?

The development of this state religion, based on humanist principles, was to have serious consequences for Christians. Whilst the State allowed for the peaceful coexistence of all religions, there was an expectation that they were to be under Caesar, the human god. This went against the fundamentals of the Christian faith in which Jesus Christ is Lord over all. Christians who refused to bow down to the State and Caesar were severely persecuted. There were even times of genocide.

HOW THE EARLY CHURCH BROUGHT DOWN THE ROMAN EMPIRE'S CULTURE

So the early Church existed in the context of a civic religion in which Caesar declared himself a god and where, much like today, society was corrupt and cruel, with sexual immorality, drunkenness, orgies, greed, ruthlessness and bloodlust.

The Gospel that was preached and lived out by the Church within this context did not simply teach forgiveness but its message of obedience and love was the means by which oppressive powers, ungodly ideologies and ways of life could be defeated and overthrown. Much of what Paul wrote in his letters to the churches was "political" in that it called on the Christians to challenge the prevailing culture. Some Christians were willing to be crucified or killed in other terrible ways rather than compromise their beliefs.

Although the New Testament writers call for social change, they do not promote civil disobedience or anarchy. As the early Christians fearlessly proclaimed the Gospel and showed people the love of God as demonstrated by community, people's hearts were changed. As their hearts were changed so the world was changed.

History shows us that Rome could cope with wars, revolutions and riots. However it could not cope with an active Christian community that that was faithful to God and His Word, whos people lived their lives in truth, love, righteousness and justice. The early Christians changed the prevailing culture of the seemingly invincible Roman Empire and replaced it with a culture based on Kingdom values. Just like the early Church we, through God's power, are able to create and cultivate a whole new culture.

THE CHURCH LOST ITS FIRST LOVE

As time passed, Christianity became very popular. Eventually the Roman Emperor himself converted to Christianity. This was the Emperor Constantine I who, in the year 313, issued an edict which stopped the persecution of Christians and introduced freedom of worship. In 380 Emperor Theodosius I made Christianity the official state religion of the Roman Empire.

Over the following centuries, the Church grew more and more powerful and became corrupt itself. For the most part, it abandoned its first love, and became motivated by the desire for power, wealth and absolute authority. There came into being Church-run states and state-run churches. The Church lost its vision of what it should be.

There have been examples in history of sometimes radical reactions against this general trend, for example, the Anabaptists, Mennonites, Moravians, Brethren and early Baptists. There have been moments of revival when the fundamental and core beliefs of the Church have been rediscovered and Jesus Christ has been re-positioned as Lord over all, and the Church has experienced renewal. Christian morality has had a major influence over the past few centuries on the shaping of Western civilisation.

However, the Church is now facing a new attack led by humanism and a civic religion.

THE CHURCH AS A MINORITY

Today the Church's influence on society has waned. The challenge the Church faces is how to live in a context where it is no longer the centre of moral authority but where it has the status of a minority.

The late Sheikh Zaki Badawi explained that Islam has no theology for living as a minority. By contrast Christianity has no theology for being a majority in society, but does have a theology for being a minority. The Church now has to rediscover how the early Church lived and to follow its model of how to survive, behave and engage in mission within a context of religious and cultural pluralism, under the power of a humanist state, within a humanist-based culture and in the presence of a powerful civic religion which is challenging the Church's very existence.

Sadly, faced with these choices, the modern Church has usually either sought to embrace the prevailing culture or removed itself from society completely thus becoming irrelevant. In both responses it has not just compromised but has denied Jesus Christ as Lord overall and failed to fulfil the fundamental purpose of its existence, that is, to spread the Gospel and to extend the Kingdom of God.

As a result the Church in the West is facing decline. It is difficult to see how the Church will survive in countries where secularism, humanism, and the rise of the new civic religion are so prevalent and the Church so compromised.

The questions we need to ask are: How should we respond? And is there hope?

Some would argue that Christians need to challenge the secular powers and to reclaim those privileges which have been lost in recent years. They believe that the gradual erosion of faith and ethics needs to be reversed and that the State should yield to Christian requirements.

But others would ask why the State should favour Christians above other peoples. It can be argued that the State represents all who live within it. If Christians are currently citizens, even as minority, they should be protected as citizens. They have the same responsibilities and privileges as others – no more than that.

Perhaps a better way is to look at how the early Church lived, and to recognise that the Church is called to be in the world but not of the world. We, as Christians, must expect to know the hatred of the world because we do not belong to the world but to Christ. We must recognise that our calling is to deny ourselves, to take up our crosses and, in obedience, follow Christ. We are to proclaim His message and to establish His Kingdom.

The Church began, grew and expanded in a hostile environment so we do not need to be afraid. For if we have the courage and confidence of Christ then we can overcome that world through the love and sacrifice of Christ.

GREAT OPPORTUNITY

Despite the strength of humanism at the moment, many people are turning to other religions and beliefs to fill the moral, spiritual and identity vacuum in their lives. Mysticism, spiritualism, paganism, the occult, Buddhism and Hinduism are all attracting large numbers of people disillusioned by their current way of living but not able to find answers in today's Church. Islam, in particular, is reaching out to a younger generation desperate for identity, meaning and guidance for their lives. Islam provides a sense of belonging, a cause, a proclamation, a community, and a set of rules for living. Islam is the fastest growing religion in the world.

The Church today faces a great opportunity. Humanism and the advance of the information age have created a world where individuals feel lost. With so much information and so many opinions available, there is a growing thirst among many people, especially young people, to know what is truly right and wrong and where they belong. The Church can use the three steps of **Creed, Community and Commandments** to meet those needs and become relevant to seeking and desperate people.

CRITICAL MOMENT IN CHURCH HISTORY

The Church stands at a critical juncture in its history. It has a choice: it can either surrender to the humanist world or reform itself. If it surrenders, the ideologies of humanism and Islam will soon dominate many parts of the world. In some parts of the Western world, where the civic religion dominates, Christianity will be reduced to small, scattered groups of faithful and uncompromised believers.

But wherever a remnant continues to exist that remains faithful to God and His commandments there is life and hope. There have been times in the past when Christianity reached a low ebb. In the Middle Ages, the Church was weak and corrupt and this allowed Islam to spread swiftly across parts of the Middle East, Asia, Europe and North Africa. In Britain, during the eighteenth century, Christianity became contaminated as it surrendered to and reflected the life of an immoral and debauched nation. Yet God, being a loving God, intervened and raised up people like Wesley and Whitefield. There was a great evangelical revival that saw the transformation of the nation to one where Christian values dominated: where the Bible was taught and known, where the weak were protected, slavery was ended, and where laws were enacted that helped to bring about justice. John Wesley in particular sought to achieve this great change in British society.

The situation was not perfect and many would say this revival should have gone much further and had far greater impact on other political and social issues such as colonialism, the class system, and the large gulf between rich and poor. But, despite these missing elements, the eighteenth century evangelical revival brought about a dramatic and positive transformation of society and God's judgement was averted.

As we saw in chapter 1, Blamires, writing about England in 1963, observed that the Christian mind had been secularised, like the rest of society. He saw that this had happened despite the fact that Christians still had "a Christian ethic, a Christian practice, and a Christian spirituality". But despite retaining these three qualities Christians were rejecting "the view that sets all earthly issues within the context of the eternal, the view which relates all human problems – social, political, cultural – to the doctrinal foundations of the Christian Faith, the view which sees all things here below in terms of God's supremacy and earth's transitoriness, in terms of Heaven and Hell" (Blamires, 1963 pp. 3-4).

In a postscript to his book, Blamires (1963 pp. 189-191) speculated about the next 50 years. He expected that wider education, increasing material wellbeing and the growing emphasis on gaining such comfort and security would make Western culture grow more consciously and outspokenly secularist, like communist Russia (the Soviet Union). This, he said, would challenge Christians to become more consciously and outspokenly Christian. He wondered whether Christians would react like Russian Christians, that is, withdraw from society and cultivate their personal morality and spirituality, never criticising the godless materialism around them, so that they could co-exist with the State. Or would Christians, he wondered, deepen and clarify their Christian commitment at the intellectual and social levels too, so that they would challenge the secularist worldview and the secularist attack on personal morality? He had no fear that Christians of the future would surrender to secularism, only that they might be "gently and slyly manoeuvred" into the position of Russian Christians. He recognised that, even in 1963, it had already become difficult for Christians to challenge contemporary culture without being labelled as bigoted or intolerant.

Half a century has passed since *The Christian Mind* was published, and Blamires, now in his hundredth year, can see that things in his homeland are worse than his worst-case scenario. Humanism and secularism have eroded the Christian ethic, Christian practice and Christian spirituality that British Christians still retained in 1963. As a result Christianity is collapsing, not only in the UK, but elsewhere in northern Europe, Canada and Australasia. Most Christians are not challenging the secular system around them, but nor are they withdrawing from it to focus on their own morality and spirituality. In fact, they seem to have surrendered to it and live lives that are barely distinguishable from those of humanists.

The question remains: how will this affect countries where the Church is still strong and growing, for example, the Caribbean, USA, South-East Asia and Africa? Will the virus which has already so catastrophically reshaped Christianity in some places also infect the Church in these countries? Will the Western spirit of individualism, rationalism and materialism spread throughout the global Church? For example, the popular 'prosperity Gospel' is an indication of how closely some parts of the Church have already succumbed to materialism.

The most important question of all is whether it is possible to turn the tide.

If we are living in days like those of Jeremiah, where judgement is certain, all we can do is pray and accept the coming judgement. But if we are living in days like those of Nehemiah, we are called to spiritually rebuild society from its moral ruins. Some ideas for how to do this are set out in chapter 12.

CONCLUSION

For over 2,000 years the Church has had to navigate its way in many different situations, through periods of peace and prosperity, through periods of danger and turmoil, even through periods when the Church has been totally destroyed in certain parts of the world. The current context of the new civic religion has faced the Church before. So lessons can be learned from the early Church about how to respond in this kind of situation. For the early Church not only managed to exist in the context of the overarching power of the Roman state religion, but actually expanded rapidly during this period. Christians faced much persecution, and at times they failed, but the Church survived and grew. In this lies our model and our hope for the future. Like the early Church we must recognise that we Christians are different from society at large, not least because we have different values and a different culture. And if persecution comes because of being different from society, we must embrace that persecution, remain faithful to Christ, and be thankful in all circumstances, trusting that God will be glorified.

12
HOW GOD CAN USE YOU TO MAKE A DIFFERENCE

In earlier chapters we have seen how humanists have influenced and are still influencing society. This chapter will focus on some possible ways we can each respond to humanism in our own areas of influence.

THE WORK PLACE

Only a small proportion of Christians work in full time ministry. Many of the people in the Bible had trades: Moses and David were shepherds; Jesus was a carpenter; Paul was a tentmaker and lawyer; Luke was a doctor; Peter and many of the disciples were fishermen. They did not see a separation between the secular and the sacred. The vast majority of Christians nowadays work in the secular world. Work and ministry must not be seen as separate.

Some people call those who work in the secular world "market place pastors" while church leaders are called "pulpit pastors". Christians who work in the secular world should see this as a ministry and opportunity to further the Kingdom of God. Market place pastors can use their work environment to spread the Gospel. They often have more contact with non-Christians than many pulpit pastors do. They can spread the Gospel to colleagues, staff, customers, suppliers and people in other business sectors.

Work is Worship
The way we work and conduct business can also be a testimony to others. In the Old Testament there is a Hebrew word which is used for both work and worship. And so it is God's desire that work should be worship. Indeed all of life is worship, as reflected in the New Testament's teaching.

As we work we should feel close to God and everything we do should be to His glory. Christians in the work place must work with integrity, must be honest and trustworthy in all they do. They must stand firm on issues such as corruption and bribery. This may be hard to do in some parts of the world. Many Christians make excuses or try to justify taking or paying bribes. But the Bible says that bribery is wrong and leads to a corruption of the heart and society (Exodus 23:8; Proverbs 15:27; Ecclesiastes 7:7). Christians must also be courageous and challenge practices and work environments that are ungodly or opposed to the fundamentals of Christianity.

GENEROSITY

The Hebrew words for righteousness and generosity are closely related. It was understood in Jewish tradition that one of the fundamental aspects of righteousness is generosity. This applies to how we spend our time, resources and finance. These things are not ours but belong to God. We must give generously of our time and finance to help those in need. This can be through local churches or Christian charities. It is through our generosity that projects such as schools, clinics, orphanages and wells can be built and maintained. By looking after those in need, Christians can demonstrate the love of God to the world.

Scripture tells us that we should give priority to helping our Christian brothers and sisters. See for example Matthew 25:40 and Galatians 6:10.

EDUCATION

As we have seen, humanism has deeply infiltrated the education system at all levels. However, Christians are able to make a large difference in this sector. It is probably one of the most important sectors to be involved in as a Christian community because what children are taught moulds their worldview, belief system and way of life.

Establishment of Affordable Christian Schools

There are many Christian schools across the world. However, most of them are very expensive. The fees from Christian schools are usually used to help generate income for other church activities. Christians need to consider how to provide good Christian education at a low, affordable cost (or even free for those in great need) so that it is available to all Christian families.

Christian Education Must Be Christian

Many Christian schools are only called Christian because they were once owned or started by churches. They may have begun with a Christian focus but now have become like non-religious schools. Many Christian schools have been so influenced by humanist society and culture that they have removed Christianity from the syllabus. Some schools which have accepted students from other religious backgrounds have removed Christianity from their core so as not to offend these students. A Christian school must have a Christian syllabus, a Christian focus and ethos, Christian worship at assembly, prayer, Bible studies and other Christian activities.

Christian Parents and Local Churches Must be Involved

Not every community can afford to build or run a Christian school. However, parents and local churches can still be very involved in the existing educational system. They must be aware of what is being taught in schools. As we have seen, humanist groups try to influence how schools are run and what is taught. Secularism and secular government policies can also prohibit traditional Christian practices such as meetings of student Christian associations and prayer during assembly. Areas of a curriculum or practices that are against Christian morals and values, or that denounce or reject the existence of God must be identified and challenged.

A common practice of humanists is to provide schools with material for religious education. This is written in such a way that Jesus and God are seen as myths and Christianity is portrayed as a religion that has been invented. Parents and churches must insist that Christianity in religious education is taught by Christians and they should provide schools with suitable Christian-focused teaching material. Religious education lessons are a great opportunity for moral education, or the "teaching of virtue" as it has been called, so as to counteract moral relativism. See, for example, *Teaching Virtue: The Contribution of Religious Education* edited by Feldenhof and Thompson (2014).

Parents and church members must take an active part in school governing bodies and committees and use their positions to ensure that Christian rights and freedoms, values and morals are protected and promoted.

Churches must support the establishment of student Christian associations and encourage outreaches to schools and even host or hold Christian holiday camps. Churches and Christian businesses must invest in providing university scholarships for Christian students to study important subjects such as politics, law, business, media and education. Christians must see being a teacher as a vital ministry. It is vital to have good, well-qualified Christian teachers who are able to have a positive impact on the next generation.

SPIRITUAL DEVELOPMENT OF CHILDREN

Parents must also take an active part in their children's spiritual development. It is likely that the children will be exposed to a humanist worldview through their school, teachers, friends, peers, social media and popular media. Parents need to be aware of the world in which their children live and take active steps to encourage and instil in them a Christian worldview and Christian morals and values. This will involve setting a good example as parents first and spending quality family time together.

POLITICS

Christians and churches often see politics as a private matter or even something that is evil. Some also believe that Christians and churches must not get involved in politics but should focus on spiritual matters. However, God has called us to be good stewards of all He has placed in our care; this includes our countries and our local communities.

Christians Must be Involved in Politics

It is interesting that church leaders and government leaders are both sometimes called ministers. The word "minister" means "servant". By being involved in politics Christians can serve their fellow-citizens. The Bible is full of people that God raised to positions of importance and influence in government and politics so that they could serve their people, for example Joseph, Daniel, Deborah, Esther and David. Many people complain about how a country is run but do very little to change it. If Christians and churches are more involved in politics they can change their country for the better. They can make sure that

Christians or others are not discriminated against by laws and policies that governments influenced by a humanist ideology may try to impose. They can promote honesty and ethical practices such as stamping out bribery and corruption.

> In 2015 a pastor in the United Kingdom managed to persuade the village council to put prayer on the agenda of every meeting. The vote in favour of this change was a bare minimum, as many councillors were opposed. But after a few months it had become accepted as normal that he prays at the beginning of each council meeting.

CHRISTIANS MUST BE CONCERNED CITIZENS

Christians who are not called to be involved in politics can still take an active interest in how their country is run. They can follow important issues in the media and pray for their political leaders (1 Timothy 2:1-4). Churches and Christian groups can work together to make stands against situations that they feel are not right, are unjust or oppose Christian values. These may involve constitutional and law changes that would affect the freedom of Christians in a nation to practise their faith and express their traditional beliefs. It may surprise many Christians what a united action can do.

Christians can also take note of what is happening in other countries where Christian rights and freedoms are abused and put pressure on their governments to intervene. Church leaders should also help their congregations understand important social, political and legal issues in the light of Biblical teachings. When elections come, it may be helpful for churches to analyse the statements of various political parties and their values, principles and policies. This does not mean that a church or church leader should advise which party to vote for but the analysis should be made, and discussion promoted so that Christian voters can make informed and wise decisions.

THE LEGAL SECTOR

All Christians, whether they are lawyers or not, must be aware of laws that challenge the rights and freedoms of Christians and bring about an erosion of morality in society.

Christian lawyers should see their work as a ministry. They must use their role as lawyers to help promote and protect the rights and freedoms of Christians in their own countries and in nations where Christians may not be able to speak up for themselves because of religious persecution. Christian lawyers can form legal advocacy groups to put pressure on governments and humanist groups that are threatening the Christian way of life or are actively targeting and persecuting Christians.

Christian lawyers must also use their legal knowledge to help other Christians to be aware of their rights and the various dangers that face them so that they too can make an informed and united stand.

MEDIA

Humanists are using popular, news and social media to good effect to promote their message and way of life. In films, television, music and even news items, practices and behaviour that were considered immoral just a few years ago are now widely accepted and encouraged, while previously accepted Christian standards of moral behaviour are ridiculed or portrayed as being bad and narrow minded. Christians must take a more active stand against the negative portrayal of Christianity, Christian morals and Christians in the media. Christians must also challenge media that actively promote drunkenness, the occult, sexual promiscuity, adultery, pornography, drug and alcohol abuse. Just criticising the media is not enough. Christians often appear to be angry and judgemental when they take stands against items in the media and this does the Christian cause very little good. It would be much more effective for Christians to explain their position without too much emotion and to use informed arguments based on fact. The effects of promoting immoral behaviour on society must be explained and alternative, acceptable, healthy behaviours suggested.

Telling the Christian story

From television soap operas and thrillers, to newspaper journalism, to posts on Facebook and Twitter it's clear that the broadcast, printed and online media engage people's minds and imaginations essentially through telling stories. God is a creative God and inspires Christians to be creative. A generation of new story tellers must emerge from within the Church who are willing and able to tell stories from a Christian perspective which will promote Christian values and ways of life in a positive and engaging way to the secular world.

13
BIBLE STUDIES AND DISCUSSION QUESTIONS

This chapter provides a Bible study and a set of questions for each of the first twelve chapters in the book. You could use the questions as part of a study group or reflect on them yourself.

CHAPTER 1

INTRODUCTION – THE NEW CIVIC RELIGION

 **Read Acts 17:24-31**

As Christians we believe God created the universe and he created each one of us. We are His offspring – His sons and daughters. He loves us deeply. He is concerned that we may be too influenced by the world we live in. He is also concerned that the world has lost its way and He calls us all to repent. We may look at the world and all the evil in it at the moment and wonder how we could ever change it. However, God looks at the peoples of the world, whatever their attitude to Him, with love. He longs to see them and the world return to Him and His way of thinking. We as believers are called into God's mission to the world to save the lost and spread his Kingdom on earth. He is ruler over all things. He rules over kingdoms and cultures. We have nothing to fear in this mission. God is not far from any of us, even unbelievers. We may find people, even those who follow humanist ways of living, more receptive to the Gospel than we think.

Some questions to think about individually or discuss in a small group

1. How have you noticed the world change in your lifetime?

2. What changes do you think have been good or bad?

3. Do you think the world is a better or worse place than it was even a few years ago?

4. What do you think has caused the world to grow better or worse?

5. Do you think the Church is weaker or stronger now than in the past?

6. Do you think the Church, and even your own local church, has been negatively influenced by the culture in which you live?

7. Which parts of your own life do you think have been influenced by the secular and humanist culture of today?

8. What did you know of this new civic religion before starting this study?

9. Read Acts 17:24-31. What is God's attitude to the world?

10. What do you think our role in the world as Christians should be?

CHAPTER 2
HISTORICAL INFLUENCES ON HUMANISM

 **Read 2 Peter 2:1-22**

It is Satan's aim to rob, steal and destroy. He looks for ways to separate humankind from God. One of these ways is by bringing about false teachings and influencing false teachers. Peter warns us that there will be false teaching. He also warns us against being influenced by these teachings and teachers. We must be sure to not to be swayed by clever arguments, or attractive ideologies or life styles that do not glorify God. As Christians we believe that God has told us that some things are absolutely right and some are absolutely wrong.

The Holy Spirit guides us in how to live and reminds us of what the Lord Jesus taught us. It would be wrong for us to convince ourselves that some sinful behaviour or way of living is acceptable to God.

Some questions to think about individually or discuss in a small group

1. Are there things about God, the Church or Christianity that you were taught at school that are different from what you have learnt from the Bible or at Church?

2. In what way do you think your education or your children's education has been influenced by humanism or a humanist way of thinking?

3. In what ways can tolerance be good or bad?

4. Read 2 Peter 2. Why do you think God is so harsh about false teachers and false teaching?

5. Are there areas in your life where you feel you have been influenced by false teaching and the new civic religion?

CHAPTER 3
RECENT HISTORY OF HUMANISM

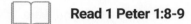 **Read 1 Peter 1:8-9**

Humanists, especially those influenced by Marxism, believe that religion causes suffering and that true happiness can only come when people are freed from religion. As Christians we disagree with this. Peter reminds us that although we cannot see Jesus we have evidence for our faith by the way we feel and experience God in our lives. The Holy Spirit places an inexplicable, supernatural joy in our hearts when we choose to believe, love and follow Jesus. Later on Peter also speaks of having tasted that the Lord is good (1 Peter 2:2-3).

Some questions to think about individually or discuss in a small group

1. The nineteenth century saw the rise of charities and human rights movements. What areas of injustice in the world today do you think the Church should try to tackle?

2. How should the Gospel play a role in the function and work of Christian social justice movements?

3. What were you taught about Darwin and his theory at school or university?

4. Did this cause you to question your beliefs?

5. Have you come across teachings or beliefs within the Church and Christian media that promote Pelagianism (the belief that humans are inherently good)?

6. Read 1 Peter 1:8-9. What experiences in your life have made you certain of your faith?

CHAPTER 4
WHAT HUMANISTS BELIEVE

 **Read Psalm 14:1-7**

David was a man who walked closely with God. He also lived among and was exposed to many cultures and nations who did not believe in God. He writes in this psalm that only a fool says in his heart that there is no God. Although humanism claims to be good, this goodness is relative. Our true goodness and righteousness come from God. If we do not believe in God there is nothing and no one to guide us as to what is right or wrong. This psalm says that people who do not believe in Him, understand Him or seek Him fall into corruption and their deeds are vile. No matter how good their intentions, people who do not believe in God bring a society to moral, social and even physical ruin.

Some questions to think about individually or discuss in a small group

1. Have you come across any of the formal elements of humanism in your community?

2. Have you seen Christianity being removed from the public space in your community?

3. Have you seen the rise of the civic religion in your community?

4. Humanists are against religion. But which aspects of humanism do you think make it a religion too?

5. It is good for the Church and the State to be separate but in what ways should the Church still influence society?

6. Read Psalm 14. Have you ever not believed in God?

7. How have things changed in your life since you have come to know the Lord?

8. What would you say to those you know who still do not believe in God?

CHAPTER 5

THE HUMANIST AGENDA

 **Read Romans 1:28-32 and Isaiah 5:20-21**

The methods and agenda of humanists are not new. They have been used for thousands of years by those opposed to God. Paul in Romans 1:32 shows that in a godless society often things that are against the will of God are not only permitted but also approved and encouraged. These verses show the consequences of such actions on society. God also warns of such actions in Isaiah 5:20-21. Shalom and peace are removed and replaced with things such as envy, strife, murder, greed, malice, gossip, disobedience and ruthlessness. This is why it so important for Christians to stand up for righteousness and justice and to oppose those who say that God does not exist.

Some questions to think about individually or discuss in a small group

1. Have you seen any reversal of norms in your community in recent years?

2. How has humanism sought to influence your society in any of the sectors mentioned above (media, education, popular culture etc.)?

3. Are there any other areas where humanism has influenced society that have not been mentioned?

4. Read Romans 1: 28-32 and Isaiah 5: 20-21. The Bible warns of the consequences of promoting a godless agenda. Have you seen the consequences of this in your own communities?

5. As Christians how should we stand against humanism and the new civic religion?

CHAPTER 6

HUMANISM, CHRISTIANITY AND SCIENCE

 **Read Psalm 111:1-10**

God has revealed Himself to us through general revelation and through special revelation. Like the psalmist when we take time out of busy lives to stop and observe the world and universe around us we will be amazed at His works. God is not only the creator of the universe, He is deeply interested in each one of us. He is a loving and just God. He is faithful and compassionate. Sometimes we do not understand Him or His ways but He invites us to think and ponder and delight in all His works. Sometimes there are things about God and His ways that are confusing. This psalm tells us that the fear (being in awe) of the Lord is the beginning of wisdom. In order to have a fear of the Lord, we must remember who God is. He is all powerful, mighty, holy. Those who fear the Lord are always aware of Him and of His love, mercy and power. They have a deep reverence and love for Him. This leads to a heartfelt commitment to obey and serve and spend time with Him. The more we spend time with God and serve Him the more we will understand His nature, and we will become wise naturally and supernaturally as the Holy Spirit leads us.

Some questions to think about individually or discuss in a small group

1. What is your attitude towards science?

2. Do you think science and Christianity should be separate?

3. How has humanism influenced your experience or understanding of God and science?

4. Do you know people who work in the scientific field and are Christians? Do you think science has strengthened or weakened their faith?

5. Read Psalm 111:1-10. How do you think God feels about humans who want to investigate His wonderful creation and understand it more (see for example, verse 2)?

6. Are there some things you are still unsure about that you should ask God or those you trust about?

CHAPTER 7
HUMANISM, CHRISTIANITY AND CREATION

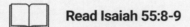 **Read Isaiah 55:8-9**

As Christians we all agree that God created the universe, the moon, the stars, the earth, plants, animals and humankind. We may disagree on how He went about this creation. The Bible is not a scientific text book but is a guide to help us find God and live according to His will. God is so big and awesome that our human minds may never be able to grasp or understand His thoughts and ways. It is good to keep seeking God through science and faith but we must be careful not to become divided as a community of believers over things we may never fully know or understand. The most important thing to hold on to is the eternal love of God as spoken about in John 3:16.

Some questions to think about individually or discuss in a small group

1. How has God revealed Himself to you generally or specifically?

2. What do you believe about how God created the universe?

3. Has this belief changed over time?

4. Has the story of creation been important to your faith journey?

5. Read Isaiah 55:8-9. What other things puzzle you about God, what He has done, or seems to not do?

6. What for you is the most important thing to believe within the Christian faith?

CHAPTER 8

WHAT HUMANISTS BELIEVE ABOUT GOD, JESUS AND THE BIBLE

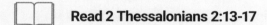 **Read 2 Thessalonians 2:13-17**

There are many verses in the Bible which call us to stand firm in our faith. Others include Philippians 1:27-28; James 5:8. Here in 2 Thessalonians 2:13-17 the Bible tells us to stand firm and hold on to the teachings that have been passed on to us through Scripture. We must not be swayed by clever arguments or by fear so that we compromise what the Bible has taught us. Humanists are very serious about their world view and life choices and may try to influence our own thinking and culture. It is important to know what the core things about the Christian faith that cannot be compromised are. Some things within Christianity are not so important to our faith, for example, the exact method God used to create the world. However, some things are core to our belief and are shared by all Christians. Christians who wish to reach out to Humanists may be tempted to downplay some of the core beliefs of the Christian faith, perhaps out of a genuine desire to do good, build relationships or show tolerance. However, we must remain true to what has been taught to us in the Bible.

Some questions to think about individually or discuss in a small group

1. Have you seen any examples of humanist ideology challenging Christian belief in your community?

2. Do you have any experience of situations where Christians have compromised the fundamentals of the Christian faith and/or are practising the new civic religion?

3. Why do you think some Christians may compromise the fundamentals of the Christian faith?

4. How can we ensure that we still hold firm to the truth in the world today?

5. Are there things not mentioned in this chapter that you feel should also not be compromised?

6. In his May 2016 blog post, Jason Allen, president of Midwestern Seminary, Kansas City, USA, suggested a number of steps which could help the Church hold on to its core beliefs. Some of these include:

    * The Church must recover the exclusivity of the Gospel
    * The Church must defend the nature and power of Scripture
    * The Church must articulate a comprehensive view of sexuality, gender and marriage
    * The Church must nurture an experiential Christianity
    * The Church must rediscover its eschatological hope
    * The Church must recover regenerate church membership

7. How can each of these areas be addressed within your own local church?

8. Read 2 Thessalonians 2:13-17. Are there areas in your life that you feel you may have compromised and where you need to reaffirm the fundamentals of the Christian faith?

CHAPTER 9

THE CHURCH AND THE WORLD

 **Read Proverbs 2**

The world is a confusing and complicated place. It is sometimes difficult to know how to live in the world and how to protect ourselves, as Christians, from the world's influences. In this chapter, Solomon, one of the wisest men who ever lived, makes a number of important observations. He says that if we obey God and hold on to His commandments, if we seek wisdom and understanding we will discover the fear and knowledge of God. This means that we will discover just how awesome and powerful God is. He is all-powerful and holy and He protects those who are faithful and righteous. If we seek Him He will help us to discern right from wrong and understand what is just and fair. He will give us wisdom and discretion to save us from the ways of wicked people and the world at large. Many people believe the adulterous woman Solomon talks about in verses 16-18 represents the evil culture in which the people lived. And so there is a promise that God's wisdom will save us from falling back into the evil ways of the world. The chapter gives a promise and a warning at the end. It says that the righteous will possess the land but the unfaithful will be torn form it.

Some questions to think about individually or discuss in a small group

1. What has challenged you most about this chapter?

2. Can you think of examples in your own life where you or your church have approached culture in each of the three ways mentioned in this chapter?

3. Are there negative aspects of culture today that you have allowed to come into your life and to influence you?

4. Read Proverbs 2. What areas of your life do you feel you need to work on to be able to understand the fear of God and find the knowledge of God?

5. Before you read the next chapter, how do think you or the Church in general should approach the world and culture?

CHAPTER 10

CREED, COMMUNITY, COMMANDMENTS

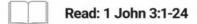 **Read: 1 John 3:1-24**

In John's first letter he starts off by encouraging us to live in community and fellowship firstly with God and then with each other. He goes on to tell us not to love the world or anything in the world. He warns against worldly beliefs and people that will try and lead us astray. But if we focus on Jesus and what He taught us we will be confident in our faith. In chapter 3 John focuses on two aspects: love and obedience. God has lavished His love on us. We are His children and have our identity in Him and as the family of believers. In a loving relationship we desire what God wants because we love Him and He loves us. We are called by God to love each other too. We must love not just with our words but also with our actions. We must meet the needs of our fellow Christian brothers and sisters. At the end of the chapter John reminds us to obey God's commandments. When we do so, we have a real and intimate relationship with our loving God. Those who obey His commandments live in Him, and He lives in them.

Some questions to think about individually or discuss in a small group

1. What do you think are the fundamental beliefs of the Christian faith?

2. Do you believe that the creed is important?

3. What would you change in your family and church to live more as the type of community God intended us to live in?

4. How do you view the relationship between love and truth in your own life?

5. How do you feel called to live out the Great Commission?

6. Read 1 John 3. In what ways have you felt God's love lavished on you?

7. Are there areas in your life that you feel you need to be more obedient to Jesus' commandments?

CHAPTER 11
A CHALLENGE TO ALL BELIEVERS

 **Read: 2 Timothy 3:10 – 4:8**

In this passage Paul speaks specifically to Timothy but generally to the Church and all believers. Paul says that everyone who wants to live a godly life in Jesus Christ will be persecuted. This is because we cannot live our lives as Christians without challenging the world's way of living. But Paul encourages us to continue in our Christian walk. We must hold on to what we have been taught in scripture which is useful for teaching, rebuking, correcting and training in righteousness. Paul tells us to preach the Word and that we must be prepared at any time to correct, rebuke and encourage others because there will be a time, such as the time we live in today, when people will reject righteousness and truth and follow their own desires. Paul urges us to show the world a better way to live through the Holy Scriptures. We must do this in love and with grace and patience but at the same time we must expect hardship and persecution. However, our reward is not in this world. As Paul says, our reward is a crown of righteousness that will be awarded to the faithful on the day of judgement. Like Paul we must be prepared to be poured out like a drink offering and must fight the good fight, finish the race and keep the faith.

Some questions to think about individually or discuss in a small group

1. Where have you noticed the Church being in decline?

2. It has been said that the Western spirit is marked by individualism, rationalism and materialism. Do you agree? To what extent are these qualities affecting the Church in your country?

3. What has been your experience of situations where Christians and churches have modelled the early Church?

4. What areas in your life and the life of your church pose the largest obstacles to transforming society?

5. Read 2 Timothy 3:10 – 4:8. In which areas of your life do you feel you are fighting the good fight?

6. Are there times you or others you know have faced persecution and hardships for living as a faithful Christian?

7. Now that you have completed this study, how do you plan to make a difference in your life, your family, community and society?

CHAPTER 12

HOW GOD CAN USE YOU TO MAKE A DIFFERENCE

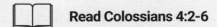 **Read Colossians 4:2-6**

The Bible teaches us to be prayerful and watchful. We must be aware of what is happening around us. We must take note of the various issues in our country, society and community that could affect us, the Christian way of life and Christian ministries. We must bring our concerns before the Lord in prayer and we must also act. We must be wise in how we deal with non-Christians and those who follow a humanist way of life. We must be strong in our faith and able to answer everyone who challenges our faith, yet still act towards them in a loving way. God can use how we react to non-Christians as an opportunity for the Gospel to be proclaimed.

Some questions to think about individually or discuss in a small group

1. How do you think God can use you to make a difference in the work place, education, politics, the legal sector or the media?

2. Are there any other areas not mentioned in this chapter where you could make a difference?

3. After learning about humanism in this book, what do you think your next actions should be within your areas of influence?

4. Which people or groups do you know that could help you achieve these planned actions?

5. Read Colossians 4:2-6. What attitudes in your own life, such as fear, insecurity or feeling that you cannot make a difference, should you pray to God about to enable you to make a stand for Christian values in your community?

Some questions to think about
membership and change in a small group

14
THE AUTHORITY OF THE BIBLE

The authority of the Bible is central to the Christian faith. The humanist declarations and manifestos do not specifically reject the Bible but they use general terms which imply the rejection of all religious texts including the Bible. The American Humanist Association is more explicit in its stand towards the Bible.

> Humanists reject the claim that the Bible is the word of God. They are convinced the book was written solely by humans in an ignorant, superstitious, and cruel age. They believe that because the writers of the Bible lived in an unenlightened era, the book contains many errors and harmful teachings.

> "Some Reasons Why Humanists Reject the Bible"
> Joseph C. Sommer, American Humanist Association

Many Christians accept the truth of the Bible simply by faith. The Holy Spirit also helps reveal the truth in the scriptures to us. However, there is also much evidence to support the validity of the Bible. Before we look at the evidence, it may be useful to explore how the Bible came to be the Bible.

HOW THE BIBLE WAS COMPILED

The basic Christian Bible consists of 66 books written over a period of about 1500 years by as many as 40 different people. As Christians we believe that all these different authors were inspired by the Holy Spirit. The first 39 books, which are the Jewish scriptures, are called by Christians the Old Testament, and were written before Christ lived on earth. (Some Christian traditions, such as Roman Catholics and Greek Orthodox, add extra books or extra chapters to the Old Testament.) The second part of the Bible consists of 27 books and is referred to as the New Testament. It was a gradual process over centuries for church leaders to decide which books were the Word of God. This list of authoritative scriptures came to be called the canon (from an Egyptian word for a measuring stick).

The first five books, which Jews call the Torah or Pentateuch, were the first to be considered as sacred. These were kept in the Ark of the Covenant. Later, various other books were added by Jewish leaders and prophets, including David and Solomon. These writings were in the form of laws, history, prophecy and poetry. These books were accepted as divinely inspired. Daniel (Daniel 9:2) refers to scripture as the word of the Lord, while Isaiah speaks of the "scroll of the Lord" (Isaiah 34:16). About 70 years after the destruction of the temple by the Babylonians in the sixth century BC, Nehemiah returned to Jerusalem to help rebuild the temple and city, and Ezra returned to preserve the scriptural and historical records of the Israelites. Ezra was a scribe and very knowledgeable about the existing scripture and law of the Lord. He was concerned that the Israelites at that time did not have access to scripture or understand scripture. In about 450 BC, he made a collection of all the existing texts and added the works of a few other writers and prophets. This may be when the Pentateuch received its present final form. He worked to restore the use of scripture in daily life amongst the people of Israel. This collection of books was widely used for centuries.

The acceptance of the Old Testament as the Word of God is confirmed by more than 4,000 direct quotes or references to the Old Testament scripture by Jesus and the writers of the New Testament.

With the exception of the writings of John, the New Testament had been completed by 70 AD. By the end of the first century the four gospel books and the epistles, or letters, were circulating amongst the early Church. Church leaders were careful to examine the authority and accuracy of the various documents and letters. The process of accepting which books should be considered scriptural took much time and consultation. A collection of books regarded as inspired by God began to circulate amongst the believers. These were written by people who either knew Jesus personally or in the case of people such as Luke and Paul were close to those who knew him. However, there were a number of heretical movements that were making use of writings which were inconsistent with the teachings of Jesus as well as with the themes and character of God shown in the Old Testament. Some such documents are the Gospel of Thomas and the Apocalypse of Peter. When these books were compared to other writings it became apparent which books were to be accepted and which ones should be rejected.

Many people believe it was not until Church leaders met for Council of Nicea in 325 AD that the Church decided which books should be included in the New Testament. The Council met to discuss a number of doctrinal issues and to confirm the core beliefs of Christianity. The Nicene Creed was one outcome of the meetings (see chapter 15). However, most of the content of the New Testament had already been agreed upon before this time although it is difficult to say exactly when.

At the end of the first century Clement of Rome, who was one of the early Church leaders and knew many of the apostles, used direct quotes or referred to more than half the New Testament books and even called them scripture. The first person to try to compile a list of canonical books was Marcion of Sinope, who was a heretic. This may have been around 140 AD. As a reaction to Marcion's efforts, church leaders felt that they should decide once and for all which of the documents were the Word of God. There is a fragment of manuscript, known as the Muratorian

Canon, which some scholars say dates from the late second century; it lists 22 of the 27 books which were later agreed to comprise the New Testament. In the late second century Irenaeus of Lyons wrote against the false teachings that were emerging at the time especially the Gnostic beliefs. He uses more than a thousand passages from all but a few New Testament books. Tertullian (155-240 AD) from Carthage, North Africa, was a prolific Christian writer and he wrote extensively and commented on most of the New Testament. These works suggest that the books of the New Testament had been decided upon by the Church by the second century. However it is only in the third century that a list of all 27 books of the New Testament is mentioned by Origen. He also writes extensively upon almost all these books creating one of the earliest commentaries. This list was later used by Athanasius in 367 AD confirming that no books had been added or removed between the third and fourth centuries. This collection of books now serves as the Christian New Testament.

With such a complicated history of how the Bible was compiled, and some uncertainty amongst scholars about the exact dates, many may question the authority and accuracy of the Bible and whether or not it is the inspired Word of God. Some may also ask if it has been amended or changed over the years to conform to Christian beliefs and traditions. There are a number of tests that can be done to assess the authenticity of the Bible. The three main tests are called the bibliographical, the external and the internal tests

BIBLIOGRAPHICAL TEST

The bibliographical test is a common tool used by historians when examining the validity of an ancient manuscript. Manuscripts and documents become decayed and have to be copied, or transcribed, from time to time to preserve them. Sometimes those doing the copying make mistakes, or things are added or left out, as copies are made over centuries. Historians look at the earliest discovered manuscripts; the time between the writing of the original manuscript and the date the discovered manuscript was written; the number of copies that exist of the earliest manuscripts; how much has changed in the manuscripts over time; and how these findings compare to other works by other writers.

Author	Book	Date written	Earliest manuscript in existence	Gap in years between writing and earliest known manuscript	Number of copies of manuscript in existence
Homer	Iliad	710-760 BC	3rd century BC	440-500	1000+
Plato	Tetralogies	During his lifetime (approx. 424 -348 BC)	895 AD	1250-1300	250
Julius Caesar	Gallic Wars	50-46 BC	Early 9th century AD	875-900	246
Livy	History of Rome	Started in 30s BC, completed in 9 BC	3rd century AD	250-310	90+
Tacitus	Annals	Completed 116/7 AD	850 AD (Books 1-6) and 1038-55 AD (Books 11-16)	750	33
	New Testament	45-97 AD	120-130 AD (part of John's gospel), late 1st century AD (Paul's letters)	70-80	5500 Greek, 350 Syriac, almost 1000 Coptic, 10,000+ Latin, 600+ Ethiopian. Total: 20,000+ (including other languages such as Slavonic, Georgian, Armenian)

It is interesting to compare how the Bible stands up against other accepted works as shown in the following table. The dates and figures are estimated, based on the work of various scholars.

This table shows that based on the bibliographical test the New Testament is the most accurately copied piece of ancient literature in the world. The difference between the time of writing and the first copies of found manuscripts is only a few decades. This is much less than the gap of hundreds of years, and in some cases more than a thousand years, for secular manuscripts. In addition, the numbers of early New Testament manuscripts hardly compares to the other secular documents. More than 20,000 copies of early New Testament manuscripts have been found in numerous languages whereas only a few hundred copies have been found of other documents. Another compelling fact is that only a 0.5% discrepancy has been found between the early manuscripts and later copies of the New Testament. It is important to note that these discrepancies are small and usually appear to be copying errors rather than theological differences. Christian historians argue that if bibliographical testing is used to accept secular works then the same testing shows that the evidence for the accuracy and authenticity of the New Testament is overwhelming.

The bibliographical test can be used for the Old Testament for which there is even more bibliographical evidence with more than 64,000 early manuscripts discovered, some dating back as far as 300 BC. There are very few errors or differences between documents that are thousands of years apart in age. Like the New Testament, there is only about 0.5% discrepancy between the various manuscripts. This is remarkable given that some books were written thousands of years ago. The differences amount to a few spelling or typographic errors. There is not a single discrepancy which changes the meaning of the Bible. No other work or piece of literature has shown such consistency.

Further proof comes from archaeological finds such as the Dead Sea scrolls. The first set of scrolls was discovered in a cave by a Bedouin goat herd boy in 1947. Between 1947 and 1956 more than 980 documents and about 60,000 manuscript fragments were discovered in nearby caves.

These documents were mostly written on leather and date from 250 BC to 68 AD. They were written in Hebrew, Aramaic and Greek, including parts of the Bible, prayers and legal documents. Bronze coins found with the manuscripts are from 135-104 BC which helps confirm the age of the scrolls. The scrolls contain fragments of almost every book in the Old Testament, including complete copies of Isaiah, the books of Samuel, and Habakkuk. When these manuscripts were compared to Bible copies made in the eleventh century AD the similarities were remarkable, with only a few spelling or word order differences or missing phrases. Most modern Bibles make mention of these and other differences between manuscripts for, example Isaiah 53:11.

Not only does the Bible stand up to the rigours of the bibliographical text, but also the evidence shows that the Bible is the most accurately and widely distributed ancient text ever written.

EXTERNAL PROOF TEST

The external proof test is used to see if there is any historical or external proof of some of the events, places or people mentioned in the text. The more external sources that confirm events, places or people the more reliable the text is considered.

When the external proof test is applied to the Bible there is overwhelming evidence which supports many other things mentioned in the Bible. Whole libraries and museums are dedicated to displaying the vast amount of external evidence that has been collected. It would be impossible in this section to deal adequately with all the external evidence that exists. The reader is urged to conduct further research on their own.

Archaeological evidence

Many sceptics of the Bible argue that the Bible was forged or written later and many of the events and personalities in it are fictitious. However, there are tens of thousands of archaeological finds and digs which support the validity of the Bible. Below are just a small fraction of some of these discoveries.

In 2005 an archaeological team lead by Dr Eilat Mazar believed they discovered the ruins of an ancient palace in Israel. Amongst many interesting historical discoveries they found small clay discs, called bullae, which were used as seals for important documents. One seal bears the name of Jehuchal Ben Shelemiah. Jehuchal Ben Shelemiah was a messenger of King Zedekiah and is mentioned twice in the Bible, Jeremiah 37:3 and 38:1-4. Another seal was found bearing the name of Gemariah Ben Shaphan, who is believed to be the secretary of King Jehoiakim as mentioned in Jeremiah 36:10. Yet another seal was found with the name Azariah Ben Hilkiah, who Dr Mazar believes is the Azariah who was one of the high priests mentioned in 1 Chronicles 9:11.

These bullae are not the only seals to have been discovered in the Holy Land. The following are just a few others which have been discovered.

Name on Bulla or Seal	Date Found	Believed to Correspond to Bible Character
Jaazaniah, servant of the king	1932	Jeremiah 40:8; 2 Kings 25:23
Shebna, servant of the king	1968	Isaiah 22:15-19; 2 Kings 18:13-37.
Azariah, son of Hilkiah	1982	Ezra 7:1; 1 Chronicles 6:13
Gemariah, son of Shaphan	1982	Jeremiah 36: 10-27
Elishama, son of Semachiah	1982	Jeremiah 36:12,20-21; 41:1; 1 Chronicles 26:7

Often sceptics believe that the Bible is false because some of the places and events mentioned in the Bible do not exist anymore. For example, the Bible mentions the Hittites many times. It was long thought that that this was invented as there was no evidence that the Hittites had ever existed. However, in 1871 archaeological digs found evidence of the Hittites and their dwellings and culture spanning more than 1200 years. Other cities whose ancient remains have been discovered include Haran, Hazor, Dan, Megiddo, Samaria, Shiloh, and Beersheba.

The city of Jericho is another example. Ancient Jericho was found in the late nineteenth century. What is interesting about this discovery is that the city had been destroyed and the walls had collapsed due to a single calamity or event such as an earthquake in about 1400 BC. The date and evidence are consistent with the events as described in the book of Joshua. John Garstang, a British archaeologist, systematically and scientifically examined the site over a period of six years (1930-1936) and concluded:

In a word, in all material details and in date the fall of Jericho took place as described in the Biblical narrative. Our demonstration is limited, however, to material observations: the walls fell, shaken apparently by earthquake, and the city was destroyed by fire, about 1400 B.C. These are the basic facts resulting from our investigations. The link with Joshua and the Israelites is only circumstantial but it seems to be solid and without a flaw.

Garstang was heavily criticised for his conclusions with many sceptics denying that the city could be linked to the events as described in Joshua. A British archaeologist, Kathleen Kenyon, was asked to conduct an independent examination of the site. She led excavations between 1952 and 1958 and agreed that the city walls had suddenly collapsed.

Archaeological finds also support some of the people and places described in the New Testament. Paul writing from Corinth says in Romans 16:23, "Erastus, who is the city's director of public works, and our brother Quartus send you their greetings." In 1929 a first century pavement in Corinth was discovered which states "Erastus, procurator and treasurer, laid this pavement at his own expense." Other discoveries include: the synagogue in Capernaum (mentioned in Mark 1:21-22 and Luke 4:31-36); the pool of Bethesda (John 5: 1-15); the pool of Siloam (John 9: 1-7); an inscription in Caesarea which reads "To Tiberius, Pontius Pilate, Prefect of Judea"; and the tomb of Caiaphas the high priest who condemned Jesus.

Mentions of Jesus and Events of the Early Church by Other Writers
Not only do archaeological finds support the validity of the Bible, but also there are many examples of Jesus being mentioned in non-Biblical texts. The following are considered authentic examples.

Irenaeus of Lyons was a student of Polycarp, who had been a disciple of the apostle John. Around 180 AD Irenaeus wrote down what Polycarp had told him about the how the gospels were written:

> Matthew published his gospel among the Hebrews in their own tongue, when Peter and Paul were preaching the gospel in Rome and founding the church there. After their departure, Mark, the disciple and interpreter of Peter, himself handed down to us in writing the substance of Peter's preaching. Luke, the follower of Paul, set down in a book the gospel preached by his teacher. Then John, the disciple of the Lord, who also leaned on His breast himself produced his gospel, while he was living at Ephesus in Asia.

Tacitus (approximate dates 55-120 AD), a Roman historian, provides one of the earliest non-Christian references to Jesus. It is of great historical value as it mentions Jesus and his death at the hands of Pontius Pilate. It also describes the early Church and the hatred and persecution that Christians endured, including from the Emperor Nero who accused them of starting the fire in Rome for which he himself was being blamed:

> Hence to suppress the prevailing rumour, he transferred the guilt upon fictitious criminals: he subjected to most exquisite tortures, and doomed to executions singularly cruel, those people who, for their detestable crimes were already in truth universally abhorred, and known to the vulgar by the name of Christians. The founder of this name was Christ, one who, in the reign of Tiberius, suffered death as a criminal, under Pontius Pilate, imperial procurator of Judea, and for a while the pestilent superstition was quelled, but it revived again and spread . . .

Josephus, a Jewish historian born in 37 AD, made mention of Jesus in two different works. Many people believe that one work was amended slightly and so there is some doubt about its reliability. However, the second work is widely regarded as genuine. The section in the second work is as follows:

> But the younger Ananus who, as we said, received the high priesthood, was of a bold disposition and exceptionally daring; he followed the party of the Sadducees, who are severe in judgment above all the Jews, as we have already shown. As therefore Ananus was of such a disposition, he thought he had now a good opportunity, as Festus was now dead, and Albinus was still on the road; so he assembled a council of judges, and brought before it the brother of Jesus the so-called Christ, whose name was James, together with some others, and having accused them as law-breakers, he delivered them over to be stoned.

Pliny the Younger was the Roman administrator of Bithynia and a prolific letter writer. Around the year 112 AD he wrote about the Christians he had been ordered to execute. In a letter to Trajan, the emperor at the time, he asks if he should continue to kill the Christians as there were so many of them. He writes of their faith and customs:

> They affirmed, however, the whole of their guilt, or their error, was, that they were in the habit of meeting on a certain fixed day before it was light, when they sang in alternate verses a hymn to Christ as to a god, and bound themselves to a solemn oath, not to perform any wicked deed, never to commit any fraud, theft or adultery, never to falsify their word . . .

The Jewish Talmud is a commentary on Jewish laws that was written between 100 and 500 AD. It contains a passage about the death of Jesus, which does not deny His existence, and even implies He performed miracles. The passage, probably written in the second century, confirms the time and method of His death. The word "hanging" in the context of this passage refers to crucifixion, just as it does in Acts 5:30 and Galatians 3:13:

Jesus was hanged on Passover Eve. Forty days previously the herald had cried, "He is being led out for stoning, because he has practiced sorcery and led Israel astray and enticed them into apostasy. Whosoever has anything to say in his defence, let him come and declare it." As nothing was brought forward in his defence, he was hanged on Passover Eve.

INTERNAL TEST

Another test which can be done to check the authenticity of the Bible is to examine the text itself for inconsistencies and inaccuracies. This is called the internal test. One of the easiest ways is to look at the overall message of the Bible. Despite having so many different authors over many centuries there is a consistent and coherent overall message throughout the Bible, which is that God created us, He loves us and desires us to have a relationship with Him.

Prophecies about Jesus

The Old Testament contains many prophecies regarding the coming Messiah. What is remarkable is that despite authors being separated by distance and time, these prophecies were all fulfilled by Jesus. There are over 300 prophecies about Jesus in the Old Testament written hundreds of years before His birth. The table below outlines just some of these.

Event	Old Testament Prophecy	Fulfilled
Born of a Virgin	Isaiah 7:14	Matthew 1:18; Luke 1:34-35
From the tribe of Judah	Genesis 49:10	Luke 3:23-33
From the house of David	Isaiah 9:6-7; 16:5; Psalm 89:35-37; 132:11; 138:1-6; 2 Samuel 7:12, 1 Chronicles 17:11; Jeremiah 23:5-6;	Matthew: 1:6,16: Luke 1:32; 3:23-31:

Born in Bethlehem	Micah 5:2	Matthew 2:1; Luke 2:4-7
Had to flee to Egypt	Hosea 11:1; Numbers 24:8	Matthew 2:14-15
Rachel weeps for her children	Jeremiah 31:15	Matthew 2:16-18 (Herod kills children)
Will perform miracles and healings	Isaiah 35:5-7	Various places in all four Gospels
Will be rejected	Isaiah 53:3	Matthew 27:20-25; Mark 15:8-14; Luke 23:18-23; John 19:14-15
Will enter Jerusalem on a donkey	Zechariah 9:9	Matthew 21:1-11
Will be betrayed for 30 pieces of silver	Zechariah 11:12-13	Matthew 26:15; 27:3-10
Will remain silent in front of His accusers	Isaiah 53:7	Matthew 26:26-63; 27:12-14
Will be killed	Isaiah 53:5-9	Matthew 27:50; Mark 15:37-39; Luke 23:46; John 19:30
Will be numbered with criminals	Isaiah 53:12	Matthew 27:38; Mark 15:27; Luke 23:32-33
His hands and feet will be pierced	Psalm 22:16	Luke 23:33; 24:36-39; John 19:18; 20:19-27
People will gamble for His clothes	Psalm 22:18	Matthew 27:35; Mark 15:24; Luke 23:34; John 19:23-24
Legs not broken during crucifixion	Psalm 22:17; 34:20	John 19:31-36
Will ascend to heaven	Psalm 68:18	Luke 24:51: Acts 1:9

Other Prophecies

Many other Old Testament prophecies have also been fulfilled. Ezekiel in Chapter 26 describes how the Phoenician city of Tyre would be attacked by many nations and destroyed. The walls and towers would be broken down, its stones, timber and rubble thrown into the sea. The city would be covered by water and fishermen would cast their nets over where the city used to be. History records that Tyre was attacked by many nations including the Egyptians, Assyrians, Babylonians, Persians and finally the Macedonians under Alexander the Great. It was eventually Alexander who sacked the city and threw the rubble into the sea to create a bridge to reach an island part of Tyre. Tyre is also famous for having many underwater ruins. Other similar prophecies have been fulfilled including Sidon (Isaiah 23; Jeremiah 27:3-6; 47:4) and Babylon (Jeremiah 50 and 51; Isaiah 13:19-22).

Reliability of the Writers and Early Christians

All the books of the New Testament were written by eye witnesses or by those who personally knew eye witnesses. Luke is very clear about how he carefully researched and questioned those who were eye witnesses.

Many have undertaken to draw up an account of the things that have been fulfilled among us, just as they were handed down to us by those who from the first were eyewitnesses and servants of the word. With this in mind, since I myself have carefully investigated everything from the beginning, I too decided to write an orderly account for you, most excellent Theophilus, so that you may know the certainty of the things you have been taught. (Luke 1: 1-4)

Paul, in 1 Corinthians 15:3-8, states that there were over 500 witnesses to resurrected Jesus. By saying that many of these witnesses are still alive, he invites his readers to question these witnesses themselves. Other references to eyewitness accounts include:

- *For we did not follow cleverly devised tales when we made known to you the power and coming of our Lord Jesus Christ, but we were eyewitnesses of His majesty (2 Peter 1:16)*

- *What we have seen and heard we proclaim to you also, so that you too may have fellowship with us; and indeed our fellowship is with the Father, and with His Son Jesus Christ (1 John 1:3)*

- *This Jesus God raised up again, to which we are all witnesses (Acts 2:32)*

- *Put to death the Prince of life, the one whom God raised from the dead, a fact to which we are witnesses (Acts 3:15)*

- *We are witnesses of all the things He did both in the land of the Jews and in Jerusalem. They also put Him to death by hanging Him on a cross. God raised Him up on the third day and granted that He become visible, not to all the people, but to witnesses who were chosen beforehand by God, that is, to us who ate and drank with Him after He arose from the dead (Acts 10:39-41)*

- *God raised him from the dead, and for many days He was seen by those who came up with him from Galilee to Jerusalem. They are now His witnesses to our people. (Acts 13:30-31)*

What is remarkable is that all of these different accounts as recorded by the nine different writers of the New Testament are consistent with each other. There may be some chronological differences in the accounts, which may have been due to theological or thematic necessity, but they do not contradict each other in any way.

The Bible is Very Honest
The Bible does not shy away from awkward facts. Many heroes of the Bible are shown to be fallible and human. Their sins and weaknesses are not hidden. For example, Moses is shown to be a murderer while David is an adulterer and murderer. The disciples are seen to be ambitious, fearful, ignorant, doubting, and prejudiced. They also argue with each other, abandon Jesus and deny Him. Another interesting point is that if the writers of the New Testament had been lying about the resurrection of Jesus and invented the story they would have surely said that the empty tomb and the risen Jesus in the garden were seen by men. Instead they

write that it was women who first saw the resurrected Jesus. Women, in those days, were considered second class citizens and their testimony often thought to be unreliable.

The Cost of Being a Follower of Christ

Further evidence of the validity of the eye witness claims is that, despite being heavily persecuted and often tortured and put to death in the cruellest ways, none of the writers denied their claims. The disciples, who were afraid and in hiding immediately after Jesus' death, became bold and began preaching the Gospel in public. This not only points to the validity of their claims but also to the power of the Holy Spirit which was given to them on the Day of Pentecost. The disciples were compelled by the Holy Spirit to preach the truth of the Gospel in extremely dangerous situations and were imprisoned and put to death because of this.

According to tradition, almost all the apostles died as martyrs. For example, Peter was crucified upside down; Andrew was also crucified (he lived for two days on the cross during which time he preached to passers-by); James, son of Zebedee, was killed with a sword; Thomas was speared to death; James, at the age of 94, was beaten and stoned to death. It would be highly unlikely for people to make up claims about Jesus and to continue to hold on to these claims in the face of torture and death. It is interesting to consider that the disciples were not killed for what they believed but for what they had seen with their own eyes.

Not only did the apostles face persecution but so too did many other early believers. In an effort to suppress the growing Church the Romans mounted a systematic campaign of persecution. Christians were stoned, thrown to lions, burnt alive, boiled in oil or skinned alive amongst many other terrible deaths. Christians accepted these tribulations peacefully and did not respond with violence. Instead of the Church being destroyed it continued to grow and spread across the world.

15
TWO CHRISTIAN CREEDS

The Apostles' Creed

I believe in God, the Father almighty,
creator of heaven and earth.

I believe in Jesus Christ, his only Son, our Lord.
He was conceived by the power of the Holy Spirit
and born of the Virgin Mary.

He suffered under Pontius Pilate,
was crucified, died, and was buried.

He descended to the dead.
On the third day he rose again.
He ascended into heaven,
and is seated at the right hand of the Father.
He will come again to judge the living and the dead.

I believe in the Holy Spirit,
the holy catholic* Church,
the communion of saints,
the forgiveness of sins,
the resurrection of the body,
and the life everlasting.

Amen

The Nicene Creed

We believe in one God,
the Father, the Almighty,
maker of heaven and earth,
of all that is, seen and unseen.

We believe in one Lord, Jesus Christ,
the only Son of God,

eternally begotten of the Father,
God from God, Light from Light,
true God from true God,
begotten, not made,
of one Being with the Father.
Through him all things were made.

For us and for our salvation
he came down from heaven:
by the power of the Holy Spirit
he became incarnate from the Virgin Mary,
and was made man.

For our sake he was crucified under Pontius Pilate;
he suffered death and was buried.
On the third day he rose again
in accordance with the Scriptures;
he ascended into heaven
and is seated at the right hand of the Father.

He will come again in glory to judge the living and the dead,
and his kingdom will have no end.

We believe in the Holy Spirit, the Lord, the giver of life,
who proceeds from the Father and the Son.
With the Father and the Son he is worshiped and glorified.
He has spoken through the Prophets.
We believe in one holy catholic* and apostolic Church.
We acknowledge one baptism for the forgiveness of sins.
We look for the resurrection of the dead,
and the life of the world to come.

Amen

*In these creeds the word "catholic" means "worldwide". It refers to the whole
Church in every place, not just to the Roman Catholic Church.

GLOSSARY

Agnostic	A person who does not know whether or not there is a God
Atheist	Someone who believes God does not exist
Canon	The list of scriptures accepted as being the authoritative Word of God i.e. the Bible
Canonical	Accepted as authoritative, divinely inspired scriptures
Capitalism	An economic or political system where trade and industry are controlled by private individuals and organisations rather than a state. The main purpose of trade and industry is to make a profit.
Carvaka	An variation of the Lokayata system which teaches that only the natural world exists so people must pursue happiness and pleasure as their top priority
Christendom	The "one Church, one State" system in which governments upheld and even enforced Christianity
Christian humanism	Christian humanists believe in God and Jesus but still hold many of the other doctrines of humanism such as celebration of humankind and ethical relativism (there are no absolute rights or wrongs).
Communism	A political or social system where property and positions are shared by the community. In practice this usually means they are controlled by a central body, usually the state.
Creed	A statement or declaration of beliefs

Ethical relativism	A belief that there are no absolute rights and wrongs. What is wrong for a person in one culture, situation or religion may be considered right by others in different contexts. Ethics and morals are seen as relative .
Evolution	The process by which organisms have developed gradually from earlier forms
Fascism	A political system which is governed by a dictator or strict ruling party which controls almost all aspects of civil life including trade, business, education and media. Opposition parties are banned and the government rules with absolute power. Hitler and Nazi Germany were Fascists.
Grace	Undeserved favour and forgiveness extended by God to believers
Humanism	In its broadest sense, humanism is any philosophy or teaching that emphasises the worth and dignity of human beings, seeks the welfare of the human race and rejoices in human achievements. During the Renaissance, most humanists were also Christians but, since the Englightenment, humanism has been marked by anti-religious and anti-Christian attitudes.
Ideology	Deep set ideas which form the basis of political, economic and religious theories or systems
Jesuit Order	A Roman Catholic order founded in 1534. Its primary purpose is to spread the Roman Catholic faith.
League of Nations	An international organisation established after the First World War to deal with global issues such a poverty, health and refugees. It was the forerunner of the United Nations.
Lokayata	An unorthodox type of Hinduism, teaching a very materialistic attitude to life, with the emphasis on the here and now

Marxism	A political and economic philosophy, system and theory founded by Karl Marx (1818-1883). Marxists oppose capitalism which they say marginalises the poor. Instead all property, trade and industry are to be centrally controlled and distributed to promote equality.
Moral relativism	See Ethical relativism
Natural law	Human knowledge about what is ethically good behaviour that can be gained simply by using human reason without needing any revelation from God
Naturalism	A theory or belief that everything has a natural cause or origin. Naturalists do not believe that God or the supernatural exist or have been involved in any aspect of the universe.
Non-theism	Religions that do not believe in the existence of God or gods. For example Theravada Buddhism
Pluralism	A culture or system where many different views and beliefs co-exist and it is accepted that each holds elements of truth that cannot be questioned.
Postmodernism	A way of thinking in which there are no absolute truths, rights or wrongs and there is tolerance of other views and beliefs without question.
Propagation	The act of spreading a view, system or belief
Relativism	See ethical relativism
Religious humanism	Religious humanists practice humanism as a religion. They meet regularly and hold humanist rituals. They have ordained leaders who perform humanist ceremonies such as weddings and funerals. Some religious humanists believe in God. Some are universalists.
Renaissance	A revival of education, art, science and literature in Europe in the fourteenth to sixteenth centuries.

Scepticism	Not taking things at face value. Proof and evidence is required before something is to be believed.
Secular humanism	This is a branch of humanism with an even stronger focus on removing all religion and God from society.
Secularism	A belief that religion and state functions must be separate from each other. Religion should be removed from the public space, for example removal of prayers in government schools.
Shalom	Shalom is a Jewish term which literally means peace. The concept of shalom is not just the absence of conflict. It refers to wholeness, harmony, completeness, tranquillity, a peace within ourselves, as well as peace with God and the peace that comes from living in good relations with others.
Socialism	A political and economic theory where the state regulates and controls the major industries and civil functions. Welfare of citizens is paramount with a focus on health and education.
Stalinism	The political ideology and system similar to communism developed by the Soviet leader Joseph Stalin (1879-1953) which is based on a state's total control of all aspects of civil life.
Theism	A religion that believes in God, gods or the supernatural.
Triune	Three in one
Universalism	Belief that there are many religions or paths which lead to God and salvation
Utopia	An imaginary ideal place where everything is perfect. "Utopia" was the name of a book written by the Biblical humanist Sir Thomas More in 1516 about a fictional island in the Atlantic Ocean. The word means "nowhere".

REFERENCES AND SOURCES

Allen, Jason K. (2016) "Seven Theological Issues Confronting Local Church". May 4. http://jasonkallen.com/2016/05/seven-theological-issues-confronting-the-local-church/ (viewed 4 May 2016).

Augustine (413-26) De Civitate Dei [City of God], Book 1, chapter 9.

Berdyaev, Nicholas (1933) The End of our Time. New York: Sheed and Ward, 54.

Blamires, Harry (1963) The Christian Mind. London: SPCK.

Boot, Joseph (2014) The Mission of God: A Manifesto of Hope. St Catharines, Ontario: Freedom Press International.

de Botton, Alain (2012) Religion for Atheists: A Non-Believer's Guide to the Uses of Religion. London: Penguin Books.

Bowman, R. (1988) "The New Puritanism: A Preliminary Assessment of Reconstructionism". Christian Research Journal 10:3.

Bready, J. Wesley (1938) England Before and After Wesley: the Evangelical Revival and Social Reform. London: Hodder and Stoughton.

Burnside, Jonathan (2011) God, Justice and Society Oxford: Oxford University Press, 68.

Cantwell Smith, Wilfred (1962 The Meaning and End of Religion. New York: Macmillan.

Cupitt, Don (1984) The Sea of Faith. London: British Broadcasting Corporation.

Dawkins, Richard (1976) The Selfish Gene. Oxford: Oxford University Press, 203-215.

Dawkins, Richard (2006) The God Delusion. London: Bantam Press.

Dunphy, J. (1983) "A Religion for A New Age". The Humanist, Jan/Feb, 26.

Edwards, Joel (2006) "The Rise of Islam". Christianity December, 18.

Edwards, Joel (2008) An Agenda for Change: A Global Call for Spiritual and Social Transformation. Grand Rapids: Zondervan.

Eidelberg, Paul (1977) Beyond Détente. La Salle: Sherwood Sugden, 74.

Felderhof, Marius and Penny Thompson (eds.) (2014) *Teaching Virtue: The Contribution of Religious Education.* London: Bloomsbury.

Furedi, Frank (2004) *Where Have All the Intellectuals Gone?* London: Continuum.

Furedi, Frank (2011) *On Tolerance: A Defence of Moral Independence.* London: Continuum.

Garstang, John. (1937) "Jericho and the Biblical Story" in J. A. Hammerton (ed.) *Wonders of the Past: The Romance of Antiquity and its Splendours.* New York: Wise & Co, 1222.

von Harnack, Adolf (1899) *History of Dogma* Vol. V. Translated by Neil Buchanan. Boston: Little, Brown and Co. 203.

Harries, Richard (2008) *The Re-Enchantment of Morality: Wisdom for a Troubled World.* London: SPCK.

Hobson, Theo (2016) "The BBC should commission a Christian version of Woman's Hour". 2 May. https://blogs.spectator.co.uk/2016/05/the-bbc-should-commission-a-christian-version-of-womans-hour (viewed 4 May 2016).

Horton, Michael S. (1994) "Heresy". *Modern Reformation* 3:1 Jan/Feb 26-32.

Irenaeus (approx. 180 AD) *Against Heresies.* 3.1.1

Josephus (93 or 94 AD) *Jewish Antiquities.* 20.9.1

Küng, Hans (1993) *Global Ethic: The Declaration of the Parliament of the World's Religions.* London: Continuum.

Küng, Hans (1995) *Christianity: Essence, History and Future.* New York: Continuum.

Layton, Richard (1997) "The Influence of Humanism in Education". http://www.humanistsofutah.org/1997/InfluenceOfHumanismInEducationTalk_8-97.html (viewed 15 April 2016).

Lewis, C.S. (1943) *The Abolition of Man, or, Reflections on Education with Special Reference to the Teaching of English in the Upper Forms of Schools.* London: Oxford University Press.

de Lubac, Henri (1944) *Le Drame de l'humanisme athée.* Paris: Spes. First English edition (1949) *The Drama of Atheist Humanism.* London: Sheed and Ward.

Marr, Andrew (2007) *A History of Modern Britain.* London: Macmillan, 254.

Marx, Karl cited by de Lubac (p. 41) as occurring in a letter from Marx to Hartmann.

Moore, Charles (2012) "Religion's usefulness is drawn from its truth". *Daily Telegraph*, 30 January.

Nietzsche, Friedrich *Der Wille Zur Macht [The Will to Power]* a posthumous collection of Nietzsche's notes. First edition 1901. Second expanded edition 1906. First English edition (1910) translated by Anthony M. Ludovici. Edinburgh and London: T. N. Foulis.

Obama, Barack (2006) *The Audacity of Hope: Thoughts on Reclaiming the American Dream*. New York: Crown Publishers.

Obama, Barack (2009) "Joint Press Availability with President Obama and President Gul of Turkey" issued by the Office of the Press Secretary of the White House, 6 April. https://www.whitehouse.gov/the-press-office/joint-press-availability-with-president-obama-and-president-gul-turkey (viewed 15 April 2016).

Pliny the Younger, Book 10, Letter 96.

Rahner, K. (1986) *Karl Rahner in Dialogue: Conversations and Interviews, 1965-1982*. Paul Imhof and Hubert Biallowons (eds), translation edited by Harvey D. Egan. New York: Crossroad, 135.

Reilly, Robert R. (1983) *Justice and War in the Nuclear Age*. Lanham, Maryland: University Press of America, Inc. 9, 16, 21.

Reiser, Oliver L. (1941) *The Humanist*, 1.

Rousseau, Jean-Jacques (1755) *Discours sur l'origine et les fondements de l'inégalité parmi les hommes [Discourse on the Origin and Foundations of Inequality among Men]*. Amsterdam: M.M. Ray. First English edition (1761) *Discourse on the Origin and Foundations of Inequality among Men*. London: R. and J. Dodsley.

Sacks, Jonathan (2011) "Has Europe Lost Its Soul to the Markets?" *The Times*, 12 December.

Samuel, Vinay (2016) Presentation at House of Commons for OCRPL launch of the book *Religious Approaches to Human Rights* by Martin Davie, 9 March.

Schlossberg, Herbert (2000) *The Silent Revolution and the Making of Victorian England*. Columbus: Ohio State University Press.

Shortt, Rupert (2016) *God is No Thing: Coherent Christianity*. London: Hurst & Company.

Solzhenitsyn, Alexander (1978) "A World Split Apart". *Vital Speeches of the Day*, September 1, 680.

Sommer, Joseph C. "Some Reasons Why Humanists Reject the Bible". *American Humanist Association* http://americanhumanist.org/humanism/Some_Reasons_Why_Humanists_Reject_the_Bible (viewed 4 May 2016)

Spurgeon, Charles Haddon (1866) *Morning by Morning, or Daily Readings for the Family or the Closet*. New York: Sheldon and Company.

Tacitus (approx. 117), *Annals* Vol. XV, 44.

The Talmud. The Babylonian Talmud, Baraitha Sanhedrin page 43 side a.

Thring, Oliver (1916) "She-devil Weldon: Rise of women drives men to change sex". *The Sunday Times,* 3 April.

Wabukala, Eliud (2016) Letter from Archbishop of Kenya to Archbishop of Canterbury, 18 March. https://www.scribd.com/doc/305733144/Letter-of-18-March-2016-From-Wabukala-to-Welby (viewed 18 May 2016)

Watson, Brenda (2014) "Being Honest" in M. Felderhof and P. Thompson (eds.) *Teaching Virtue: The Contribution of Religious Education.* London: Bloomsbury, 77.

Watson, Brenda (2014) "The Need for Responsible Religious Education in the Light of the 'Value Free' Society" in Marius Felderhof and Penny Thompson (eds.) *Teaching Virtue: The Contribution of Religious Education.* London: Bloomsbury, 30-34.

Weldon, Fay (2016). See interview by Oliver Thring.

Zubovich, Gene (2016) "The Strange Short Career of Judeo-Christianity". https://aeon.co/opinions/the-strange-short-career-of-judeo-christianity (viewed 15 April 2016).

SOURCE OF IMAGES

Page 37 – Richard Dawkins by Matthias Asgeirsson / CC BY-SA 2.0 (Flickr)
Page 38 – Stephen Fry by Beao / CC BY-SA 3.0 (Wikimedia Commons)
Page 38 – John Lennon by Roy Kerwood / CC BY 2.5 (Wikimedia Commons)
Page 38 – Salman Rushdie by David Shankbone / CC BY-SA 3.0 (Wikimedia Commons)
Page 53 – Bus with British Humanist Association Slogan by Jon Worth / CC BY 2.0 (Flickr)

All other images are public domain or owned by Isaac Publishing.

FIVE KEY HUMANIST DOCUMENTS

Humanist Manifesto I (1933)
http://americanhumanist.org/humanism/humanist_manifesto_i

Humanist Manifesto II (1973)
http://americanhumanist.org/humanism/humanist_manifesto_ii

Humanist Manifesto III (2003)
http://americanhumanist.org/humanism/humanist_manifesto_iii

Amsterdam Declaration of the World Humanist Congress 1952
http://iheu.org/humanism/the-amsterdam-declaration/the-amsterdam-declaration-1952/

Amsterdam Declaration of the World Humanist Congress 2002
http://iheu.org/humanism/the-amsterdam-declaration/

LETTER FROM U.S. DEPARTMENTS OF EDUCATION AND JUSTICE

U.S. Department of Justice
Civil Rights Division

U.S. Department of Education
Office for Civil Rights

May 13, 2016

Dear Colleague:

Schools across the country strive to create and sustain inclusive, supportive, safe, and nondiscriminatory communities for all students. In recent years, we have received an increasing number of questions from parents, teachers, principals, and school superintendents about civil rights protections for transgender students. Title IX of the Education Amendments of 1972 (Title IX) and its implementing regulations prohibit sex discrimination in educational programs and activities operated by recipients of Federal financial assistance.[1] This prohibition encompasses discrimination based on a student's gender identity, including discrimination based on a student's transgender status. This letter summarizes a school's Title IX obligations regarding transgender students and explains how the U.S. Department of Education (ED) and the U.S. Department of Justice (DOJ) evaluate a school's compliance with these obligations.

ED and DOJ (the Departments) have determined that this letter is *significant guidance*.[2] This guidance does not add requirements to applicable law, but provides information and examples to inform recipients about how the Departments evaluate whether covered entities are complying with their legal obligations. If you have questions or are interested in commenting on this guidance, please contact ED at ocr@ed.gov or 800-421-3481 (TDD 800-877-8339); or DOJ at education@usdoj.gov or 877-292-3804 (TTY: 800-514-0383).

Accompanying this letter is a separate document from ED's Office of Elementary and Secondary Education, *Examples of Policies and Emerging Practices for Supporting Transgender Students*. The examples in that document are taken from policies that school districts, state education agencies, and high school athletics associations around the country have adopted to help ensure that transgender students enjoy a supportive and nondiscriminatory school environment. Schools are encouraged to consult that document for practical ways to meet Title IX's requirements.[3]

Terminology

- ☐ *Gender identity* refers to an individual's internal sense of gender. A person's gender identity may be different from or the same as the person's sex assigned at birth.

- ☐ *Sex assigned at birth* refers to the sex designation recorded on an infant's birth certificate should such a record be provided at birth.

- ☐ *Transgender* describes those individuals whose gender identity is different from the sex they were assigned at birth. A *transgender male* is someone who identifies as male but was assigned the sex of female at birth; a *transgender female* is someone who identifies as female but was assigned the sex of male at birth.

☐ *Gender transition* refers to the process in which transgender individuals begin asserting the sex that corresponds to their gender identity instead of the sex they were assigned at birth. During gender transition, individuals begin to live and identify as the sex consistent with their gender identity and may dress differently, adopt a new name, and use pronouns consistent with their gender identity. Transgender individuals may undergo gender transition at any stage of their lives, and gender transition can happen swiftly or over a long duration of time.

Compliance with Title IX

As a condition of receiving Federal funds, a school agrees that it will not exclude, separate, deny benefits to, or otherwise treat differently on the basis of sex any person in its educational programs or activities unless expressly authorized to do so under Title IX or its implementing regulations.[4] The Departments treat a student's gender identity as the student's sex for purposes of Title IX and its implementing regulations. This means that a school must not treat a transgender student differently from the way it treats other students of the same gender identity. The Departments' interpretation is consistent with courts' and other agencies' interpretations of Federal laws prohibiting sex discrimination.[5]

The Departments interpret Title IX to require that when a student or the student's parent or guardian, as appropriate, notifies the school administration that the student will assert a gender identity that differs from previous representations or records, the school will begin treating the student consistent with the student's gender identity. Under Title IX, there is no medical diagnosis or treatment requirement that students must meet as a prerequisite to being treated consistent with their gender identity.[6] Because transgender students often are unable to obtain identification documents that reflect their gender identity (*e.g.*, due to restrictions imposed by state or local law in their place of birth or residence),[7] requiring students to produce such identification documents in order to treat them consistent with their gender identity may violate Title IX when doing so has the practical effect of limiting or denying students equal access to an educational program or activity.

A school's Title IX obligation to ensure nondiscrimination on the basis of sex requires schools to provide transgender students equal access to educational programs and activities even in circumstances in which other students, parents, or community members raise objections or concerns. As is consistently recognized in civil rights cases, the desire to accommodate others' discomfort cannot justify a policy that singles out and disadvantages a particular class of students.[8]

1. *Safe and Nondiscriminatory Environment*

Schools have a responsibility to provide a safe and nondiscriminatory environment for all students, including transgender students. Harassment that targets a student based on gender identity, transgender status, or gender transition is harassment based on sex, and the Departments enforce Title IX accordingly.[9] If sex-based harassment creates a hostile environment, the school must take prompt and effective steps to end the harassment, prevent its recurrence, and, as appropriate, remedy its effects. A school's failure to treat students consistent with their gender identity may create or contribute to a hostile environment in violation of Title IX. For a more detailed discussion of Title IX requirements related to sex-based harassment, see guidance documents from ED's Office for Civil Rights (OCR) that are specific to this topic.[10]

2. Identification Documents, Names, and Pronouns

Under Title IX, a school must treat students consistent with their gender identity even if their education records or identification documents indicate a different sex. The Departments have resolved Title IX investigations with agreements committing that school staff and contractors will use pronouns and names consistent with a transgender student's gender identity.[11]

3. Sex-Segregated Activities and Facilities

Title IX's implementing regulations permit a school to provide sex-segregated restrooms, locker rooms, shower facilities, housing, and athletic teams, as well as single-sex classes under certain circumstances.[12] When a school provides sex-segregated activities and facilities, transgender students must be allowed to participate in such activities and access such facilities consistent with their gender identity.[13]

☐ **Restrooms and Locker Rooms.** A school may provide separate facilities on the basis of sex, but must allow transgender students access to such facilities consistent with their gender identity.[14] A school may not require transgender students to use facilities inconsistent with their gender identity or to use individual-user facilities when other students are not required to do so. A school may, however, make individual-user options available to all students who voluntarily seek additional privacy.[15]

☐ **Athletics.** Title IX regulations permit a school to operate or sponsor sex-segregated athletics teams when selection for such teams is based upon competitive skill or when the activity involved is a contact sport.[16] A school may not, however, adopt or adhere to requirements that rely on overly broad generalizations or stereotypes about the differences between transgender students and other students of the same sex (*i.e.*, the same gender identity) or others' discomfort with transgender students.[17] Title IX does not prohibit age-appropriate, tailored requirements based on sound, current, and research-based medical knowledge about the impact of the students' participation on the competitive fairness or physical safety of the sport.[18]

☐ **Single-Sex Classes.** Although separating students by sex in classes and activities is generally prohibited, nonvocational elementary and secondary schools may offer nonvocational single-sex classes and extracurricular activities under certain circumstances.[19] When offering such classes and activities, a school must allow transgender students to participate consistent with their gender identity.

☐ **Single-Sex Schools.** Title IX does not apply to the admissions policies of certain educational institutions, including nonvocational elementary and secondary schools, and private undergraduate colleges.[20] Those schools are therefore permitted under Title IX to set their own sex-based admissions policies. Nothing in Title IX prohibits a private undergraduate women's college from admitting transgender women if it so chooses.

☐ **Social Fraternities and Sororities.** Title IX does not apply to the membership practices of social fraternities and sororities.[21] Those organizations are therefore permitted under Title IX to set their own policies regarding the sex, including gender identity, of their members. Nothing in Title IX prohibits a fraternity from admitting transgender men or a sorority from admitting transgender women if it so chooses.

☐ **Housing and Overnight Accommodations.** Title IX allows a school to provide separate housing on the basis of sex.[22] But a school must allow transgender students to access housing consistent with their gender identity and may not require transgender students to stay in single-occupancy accommodations or to disclose personal information when not required of other students. Nothing in Title IX prohibits a school from honoring a student's voluntary request for single-occupancy accommodations if it so chooses.[23]

☐ **Other Sex-Specific Activities and Rules.** Unless expressly authorized by Title IX or its implementing regulations, a school may not segregate or otherwise distinguish students on the basis of their sex, including gender identity, in any school activities or the application of any school rule. Likewise, a school may not discipline students or exclude them from participating in activities for appearing or behaving in a manner that is consistent with their gender identity or that does not conform to stereotypical notions of masculinity or femininity (*e.g.*, in yearbook photographs, at school dances, or at graduation ceremonies).[24]

4. *Privacy and Education Records*

Protecting transgender students' privacy is critical to ensuring they are treated consistent with their gender identity. The Departments may find a Title IX violation when a school limits students' educational rights or opportunities by failing to take reasonable steps to protect students' privacy related to their transgender status, including their birth name or sex assigned at birth.[25] Nonconsensual disclosure of personally identifiable information (PII), such as a student's birth name or sex assigned at birth, could be harmful to or invade the privacy of transgender students and may also violate the Family Educational Rights and Privacy Act (FERPA).[26] A school may maintain records with this information, but such records should be kept confidential.

☐ **Disclosure of Personally Identifiable Information from Education Records.** FERPA generally prevents the nonconsensual disclosure of PII from a student's education records; one exception is that records may be disclosed to individual school personnel who have been determined to have a legitimate educational interest in the information.[27] Even when a student has disclosed the student's transgender status to some members of the school community, schools may not rely on this FERPA exception to disclose PII from education records to other school personnel who do not have a legitimate educational interest in the information. Inappropriately disclosing (or requiring students or their parents to disclose) PII from education records to the school community may violate FERPA and interfere with transgender students' right under Title IX to be treated consistent with their gender identity.

☐ **Disclosure of Directory Information.** Under FERPA's implementing regulations, a school may disclose appropriately designated directory information from a student's education record if disclosure would not generally be considered harmful or an invasion of privacy.[28] Directory information may include a student's name, address, telephone number, date and place of birth, honors and awards, and dates of attendance.[29] School officials may not designate students' sex, including transgender status, as directory information because doing so could be harmful or an invasion of privacy.[30] A school also must allow eligible students (*i.e.*, students who have reached 18 years of age or are attending a postsecondary institution) or parents, as appropriate, a reasonable amount of time to request that the school not disclose a student's directory information.[31]

☐ **Amendment or Correction of Education Records.** A school may receive requests to correct a student's education records to make them consistent with the student's gender identity. Updating a transgender student's education records to reflect the student's gender identity and new name will help protect privacy and ensure personnel consistently use appropriate names and pronouns.

   o   Under FERPA, a school must consider the request of an eligible student or parent to amend information in the student's education records that is inaccurate, misleading, or in violation of the student's privacy rights.[32] If the school does not amend the record, it must inform the requestor of its decision and of the right to a hearing. If, after the hearing, the school does not amend the record, it must inform the requestor of the right to insert a statement in the record with the requestor's comments on the contested information, a statement that the requestor disagrees with the hearing decision, or both. That statement must be disclosed whenever the record to which the statement relates is disclosed.[33]

   o   Under Title IX, a school must respond to a request to amend information related to a student's transgender status consistent with its general practices for amending other students' records.[34] If a student or parent complains about the school's handling of such a request, the school must promptly and equitably resolve the complaint under the school's Title IX grievance procedures.[35]

* * *

We appreciate the work that many schools, state agencies, and other organizations have undertaken to make educational programs and activities welcoming, safe, and inclusive for all students.

Sincerely,

/s/   /s/

Catherine E. Lhamon   Vanita Gupta
Assistant Secretary for Civil Rights   Principal Deputy Assistant Attorney General for Civil Rights
U.S. Department of Education   U.S. Department of Justice

Dear Colleague Letter: Transgender Students

---

[1] 20 U.S.C. §§ 1681–1688; 34 C.F.R. Pt. 106; 28 C.F.R. Pt. 54. In this letter, the term *schools* refers to recipients of Federal financial assistance at all educational levels, including school districts, colleges, and universities. An educational institution that is controlled by a religious organization is exempt from Title IX to the extent that compliance would not be consistent with the religious tenets of such organization. 20 U.S.C. § 1681(a)(3); 34 C.F.R. § 106.12(a).

[2] Office of Management and Budget, Final Bulletin for Agency Good Guidance Practices, 72 Fed. Reg. 3432 (Jan. 25, 2007), www.whitehouse.gov/sites/default/files/omb/fedreg/2007/012507_good_guidance.pdf.

[3] ED, *Examples of Policies and Emerging Practices for Supporting Transgender Students* (May 13, 2016), www.ed.gov/oese/oshs/emergingpractices.pdf. OCR also posts many of its resolution agreements in cases involving transgender students online at www.ed.gov/ocr/lgbt.html. While these agreements address fact-specific cases, and therefore do not state general policy, they identify examples of ways OCR and recipients have resolved some issues addressed in this guidance.

[4] 34 C.F.R. §§ 106.4, 106.31(a). For simplicity, this letter cites only to ED's Title IX regulations. DOJ has also promulgated Title IX regulations. *See* 28 C.F.R. Pt. 54. For purposes of how the Title IX regulations at issue in this guidance apply to transgender individuals, DOJ interprets its regulations similarly to ED. State and local rules cannot limit or override the requirements of Federal laws. *See* 34 C.F.R. § 106.6(b).

[5] *See, e.g., Price Waterhouse v. Hopkins*, 490 U.S. 228 (1989); *Oncale v. Sundowner Offshore Servs. Inc.*, 523 U.S. 75, 79 (1998); *G.G. v. Gloucester Cnty. Sch. Bd.*, No. 15-2056, 2016 WL 1567467, at *8 (4th Cir. Apr. 19, 2016); *Glenn v. Brumby*, 663 F.3d 1312, 1317 (11th Cir. 2011); *Smith v. City of Salem*, 378 F.3d 566, 572-75 (6th Cir. 2004); *Rosa v. Park W. Bank & Trust Co.*, 214 F.3d 213, 215–16 (1st Cir. 2000); *Schwenk v. Hartford*, 204 F.3d 1187, 1201–02 (9th Cir. 2000); *Schroer v. Billington*, 577 F. Supp. 2d 293, 306-08 (D.D.C. 2008); *Macy v. Dep't of Justice*, Appeal No. 012012082 (U.S. Equal Emp't Opportunity Comm'n Apr. 20, 2012). *See also* U.S. Dep't of Labor (USDOL), Training and Employment Guidance Letter No. 37-14, *Update on Complying with Nondiscrimination Requirements: Discrimination Based on Gender Identity, Gender Expression and Sex Stereotyping are Prohibited Forms of Sex Discrimination in the Workforce Development System* (2015), wdr.doleta.gov/directives/attach/TEGL/TEGL_37-14.pdf; USDOL, Job Corps, Directive: Job Corps Program Instruction Notice No. 14-31, *Ensuring Equal Access for Transgender Applicants and Students to the Job Corps Program* (May 1, 2015), https://supportservices.jobcorps.gov/Program%20Instruction%20Notices/pi_14_31.pdf; DOJ, Memorandum from the Attorney General, *Treatment of Transgender Employment Discrimination Claims Under Title VII of the Civil Rights Act of 1964* (2014), www.justice.gov/sites/default/files/opa/press-releases/attachments/2014/12/18/title_vii_memo.pdf; USDOL, Office of Federal Contract Compliance Programs, Directive 2014-02, *Gender Identity and Sex Discrimination* (2014), www.dol.gov/ofccp/regs/compliance/directives/dir2014_02.html.

[6] *See Lusardi v. Dep't of the Army*, Appeal No. 0120133395 at 9 (U.S. Equal Emp't Opportunity Comm'n Apr. 1, 2015) ("An agency may not condition access to facilities—or to other terms, conditions, or privileges of employment—on the completion of certain medical steps that the agency itself has unilaterally determined will somehow prove the bona fides of the individual's gender identity.").

[7] *See G.G.*, 2016 WL 1567467, at *1 n.1 (noting that medical authorities "do not permit sex reassignment surgery for persons who are under the legal age of majority").

[8] 34 C.F.R. § 106.31(b)(4); *see G.G.*, 2016 WL 1567467, at *8 & n.10 (affirming that individuals have legitimate and important privacy interests and noting that these interests do not inherently conflict with nondiscrimination principles); *Cruzan v. Special Sch. Dist. No. 1*, 294 F.3d 981, 984 (8th Cir. 2002) (rejecting claim that allowing a transgender woman "merely [to be] present in the women's faculty restroom" created a hostile environment); *Glenn*, 663 F.3d at 1321 (defendant's proffered justification that "other women might object to [the plaintiff]'s restroom use" was "wholly irrelevant"). *See also Palmore v. Sidoti*, 466 U.S. 429, 433 (1984) ("Private biases may be outside the reach of the law, but the law cannot, directly or indirectly, give them effect."); *City of Cleburne v. Cleburne Living Ctr.*, 473 U.S. 432, 448 (1985) (recognizing that "mere negative attitudes, or fear . . . are not permissible bases for" government action).

---

[9] *See, e.g.,* Resolution Agreement, *In re Downey Unified Sch. Dist., CA,* OCR Case No. 09-12-1095, (Oct. 8, 2014), www.ed.gov/documents/press-releases/downey-school-district-agreement.pdf (agreement to address harassment of transgender student, including allegations that peers continued to call her by her former name, shared pictures of her prior to her transition, and frequently asked questions about her anatomy and sexuality); Consent Decree, *Doe v. Anoka-Hennepin Sch. Dist. No. 11, MN* (D. Minn. Mar. 1, 2012), www.ed.gov/ocr/docs/investigations/05115901-d.pdf (consent decree to address sex-based harassment, including based on nonconformity with gender stereotypes); Resolution Agreement, *In re Tehachapi Unified Sch. Dist., CA,* OCR Case No. 09-11-1031 (June 30, 2011), www.ed.gov/ocr/docs/investigations/09111031-b.pdf (agreement to address sexual and gender-based harassment, including harassment based on nonconformity with gender stereotypes). *See also Lusardi,* Appeal No. 0120133395, at *15 ("Persistent failure to use the employee's correct name and pronoun may constitute unlawful, sex-based harassment if such conduct is either severe or pervasive enough to create a hostile work environment").

[10] *See, e.g.,* OCR, *Revised Sexual Harassment Guidance: Harassment of Students by School Employees, Other Students, or Third Parties* (2001), www.ed.gov/ocr/docs/shguide.pdf; OCR, *Dear Colleague Letter: Harassment and Bullying* (Oct. 26, 2010), www.ed.gov/ocr/letters/colleague-201010.pdf; OCR, *Dear Colleague Letter: Sexual Violence* (Apr. 4, 2011), www.ed.gov/ocr/letters/colleague-201104.pdf; OCR, *Questions and Answers on Title IX and Sexual Violence* (Apr. 29, 2014), www.ed.gov/ocr/docs/qa-201404-title-ix.pdf.

[11] *See, e.g.,* Resolution Agreement, *In re Cent. Piedmont Cmty. Coll., NC,* OCR Case No. 11-14-2265 (Aug. 13, 2015), www.ed.gov/ocr/docs/investigations/more/11142265-b.pdf (agreement to use a transgender student's preferred name and gender and change the student's official record to reflect a name change).

[12] 34 C.F.R. §§ 106.32, 106.33, 106.34, 106.41(b).

[13] *See* 34 C.F.R. § 106.31.

[14] 34 C.F.R. § 106.33.

[15] *See, e.g.,* Resolution Agreement, *In re Township High Sch. Dist. 211, IL,* OCR Case No. 05-14-1055 (Dec. 2, 2015), www.ed.gov/ocr/docs/investigations/more/05141055-b.pdf (agreement to provide any student who requests additional privacy "access to a reasonable alternative, such as assignment of a student locker in near proximity to the office of a teacher or coach; use of another private area (such as a restroom stall) within the public area; use of a nearby private area (such as a single-use facility); or a separate schedule of use.").

[16] 34 C.F.R. § 106.41(b). Nothing in Title IX prohibits schools from offering coeducational athletic opportunities.

[17] 34 C.F.R. § 106.6(b), (c). An interscholastic athletic association is subject to Title IX if (1) the association receives Federal financial assistance or (2) its members are recipients of Federal financial assistance and have ceded controlling authority over portions of their athletic program to the association. Where an athletic association is covered by Title IX, a school's obligations regarding transgender athletes apply with equal force to the association.

[18] The National Collegiate Athletic Association (NCAA), for example, reported that in developing its policy for participation by transgender students in college athletics, it consulted with medical experts, athletics officials, affected students, and a consensus report entitled *On the Team: Equal Opportunity for Transgender Student Athletes* (2010) by Dr. Pat Griffin & Helen J. Carroll (*On the Team*), https://www.ncaa.org/sites/default/files/NCLR_TransStudentAthlete%2B(2).pdf. *See* NCAA Office of Inclusion, *NCAA Inclusion of Transgender Student-Athletes* 2, 30-31 (2011), https://www.ncaa.org/sites/default/files/Transgender_Handbook_2011_Final.pdf (citing *On the Team*). The *On the Team* report noted that policies that may be appropriate at the college level may "be unfair and too complicated for [the high school] level of competition." *On the Team* at 26. After engaging in similar processes, some state interscholastic athletics associations have adopted policies for participation by transgender students in high school athletics that they determined were age-appropriate.

[19] 34 C.F.R. § 106.34(a), (b). Schools may also separate students by sex in physical education classes during participation in contact sports. *Id.* § 106.34(a)(1).

[20] 20 U.S.C. § 1681(a)(1); 34 C.F.R. § 106.15(d); 34 C.F.R. § 106.34(c) (a recipient may offer a single-sex public nonvocational elementary and secondary school so long as it provides students of the excluded sex a "substantially

equal single-sex school or coeducational school").

[21] 20 U.S.C. § 1681(a)(6)(A); 34 C.F.R. § 106.14(a).

[22] 20 U.S.C. § 1686; 34 C.F.R. § 106.32.

[23] *See, e.g.,* Resolution Agreement, *In re Arcadia Unified. Sch. Dist., CA,* OCR Case No. 09-12-1020, DOJ Case No. 169-12C-70, (July 24, 2013), www.justice.gov/sites/default/files/crt/legacy/2013/07/26/arcadiaagree.pdf (agreement to provide access to single-sex overnight events consistent with students' gender identity, but allowing students to request access to private facilities).

[24] *See* 34 C.F.R. §§ 106.31(a), 106.31(b)(4). *See also, In re Downey Unified Sch. Dist., CA, supra* n. 9; *In re Cent. Piedmont Cmty. Coll., NC, supra* n. 11.

[25] 34 C.F.R. § 106.31(b)(7).

[26] 20 U.S.C. § 1232g; 34 C.F.R. Part 99. FERPA is administered by ED's Family Policy Compliance Office (FPCO). Additional information about FERPA and FPCO is available at www.ed.gov/fpco.

[27] 20 U.S.C. § 1232g(b)(1)(A); 34 C.F.R. § 99.31(a)(1).

[28] 34 C.F.R. §§ 99.3, 99.31(a)(11), 99.37.

[29] 20 U.S.C. § 1232g(a)(5)(A); 34 C.F.R. § 99.3.

[30] Letter from FPCO to Institutions of Postsecondary Education 3 (Sept. 2009), www.ed.gov/policy/gen/guid/fpco/doc/censuslettertohighered091609.pdf.

[31] 20 U.S.C. § 1232g(a)(5)(B); 34 C.F.R. §§ 99.3. 99.37(a)(3).

[32] 34 C.F.R. § 99.20.

[33] 34 C.F.R. §§ 99.20-99.22.

[34] *See* 34 C.F.R. § 106.31(b)(4).

[35] 34 C.F.R. § 106.8(b).

INDEX